Col.

easy learning

French

in a click

Sophie Gavrois

HarperCollins Publishers
77-85 Fulham Palace Road
London W6 8JB
Great Britain

www.collinslanguage.com

First edition 2010

Reprint 10 9 8 7 6 5 4 3 2 1

© HarperCollins Publishers 2010

ISBN 978-0-00-733715-6

Collins® is a registered trademark of
HarperCollins Publishers Limited

A catalogue record for this book is available
from the British Library

Typeset by Q2AMedia

Cover image courtesy of Corbis

Audio material recorded and produced by
Networks SRL, Milan

Printed and Bound in China by Leo Paper
Products Ltd.

Editorial Director: Eva Martinez

Series Editor: Rob Scriven

Contents

Introduction

Welcome to *Collins Easy Learning French in a Click*. This is a new course which aims to give you all the skills you'll need to start understanding and using French quickly, easily and effectively in real situations.

This course is aimed at adult learners with no previous experience of French. We've thought about which situations would be most useful to you during a visit to France, and have created a course that embraces all the main scenarios a traveller would be likely to encounter, such as public transport, checking into a hotel, shopping, eating out, and visiting a museum or a wine cellar.

Our approach is not to bombard you with too much grammar, but rather to let you listen to authentic dialogues set in useful situations, giving you the nuts and bolts of what's being said, then guiding you through carefully gauged practice exercises to increase your confidence.

The tools you need to succeed

The course has been designed to provide you with three essential tools in order to make your language learning experience a success. In your pack you'll find an activation code for the **online course**, this handy **book**, and an **audio CD**. You can use a combination of these whenever and wherever you are, making the course work for you.

The online course

www.collinslanguage.com/click provides you with a 12-unit online interactive language experience. Listen to a dialogue (and follow the words on-screen if you like) then study the new words and phrases before tackling some fun interactive games and exercises. You'll then also have the chance to perfect your pronunciation by recording your own voice (microphone not provided).

To access the online course simply go to www.collinslanguage.com/click and enter your personal activation code which you will find inside the front cover of this book.

The book

There will be times when it's not practical for you to be at a computer. There will also be times when you simply don't want to stare at the screen. For these times, this pocket-sized book contains the whole course for you in a handy portable format, so you can continue learning without the need for a computer. All of the content you need to learn French is right here in this book. Study the language and complete the exercises just as you would online.

When you want to check your answers, go to **www.collinslanguage.com/click** to download the answer key.

The audio CD

Use the audio CD to hear native French speakers engaging in dialogues set in real life situations and use it alongside the book in order to improve your listening comprehension skills. The audio CD can be downloaded to your mp3 player so that you can keep on learning even when you're on the move.

See the website at **www.collinslanguage.com/click** for the written transcript of all the spoken dialogues.

How it works

French in a Click is divided into 12 units with revision sections after Unit 6 and Unit 12. Each unit begins with a **Traveller's tip**, a short passage highlighting an area of French life and culture, offering you tips on what to expect when you visit the country.

Following a brief summary of the language structures you're about to study, we move straight on to the first dialogue, headed **Listen up**. Any tricky or useful vocabulary is then explained in the **Words and phrases** box (with accompanying audio online), then we go into a little more detail in **Unlocking the language**. Then it's over to you. **Your Turn** offers further practice of each structure and area of vocabulary encountered.

Halfway through each unit, you'll see that the cycle begins again with a fresh **Listen up**. This adds a different dimension to the material and scenario you've already looked at, and provides you with a new challenge in a slightly different situation.

Each unit ends with **Let's Recap**, in which you can check over the language you've used in the unit. The online version then gives you the chance to **record yourself** saying some of the most important vocabulary from the unit, to compare your pronunciation with that of a native speaker.

***Collins Easy Learning French in a Click* aims to be fun, but at the same time to equip you with genuinely useful linguistic and cultural tools to make the most of your time in France. We hope you enjoy it!**

Enchanté
Pleased to meet you

We'll look at greetings and how to introduce yourself and say where you're from. You'll also learn how to say where you're going on holiday, and for how long.

Traveller's tip

The boom in affordable flights and ferry crossings in the 1970s and 80s, and the opening of the Channel Tunnel in 1994 put France firmly on the map for foreign visitors, and its popularity continues to this day.

Paris draws in most visitors, with its cultural and night life, its numerous museums and monuments, and the *haute couture* and chic boutiques. The other regions of France attract visitors for a variety of reasons, such as wine, cuisine, architecture, history, outdoor activities or sports.

The rise of budget airlines, together with the subsequent drop in air fares, has made the French Alps and the Pyrenees, small villages and lesser known regions much more accessible to travellers. Whatever type of visit to France you're planning, you'll discover its many landscapes and specialities: from the coastlines of the Atlantic Ocean, the Channel and Mediterranean, the Champagne region in the east and the Bordeaux vineyards in the west, the sixteenth-century châteaux of the Loire Valley to the prehistoric caves of the Dordogne and Ardèche, and to the *maquis* scrubland of the south to the 'green Venice' of the Marais Poitevin in the west – these places will make you appreciate why the French usually spend their vacations in their home country.

Internal flights, trains, car hire and accommodation can be booked online, and there are many rural properties and holiday cottages to rent by the weekend, week or month. You can find more details about this type of accommodation by searching for **gîtes** and **gîtes ruraux** on the internet.

In this unit we'll be working with two useful structures, to allow us to introduce ourselves and to say where we're going.

Je suis ...   I am ...
Je vais à ...   I'm going to ...

 Listen up 1

A British woman meets a French man just before they catch a flight to Montpellier. You can follow the conversation below as you listen to it, then you'll find a series of explanations and exercises linked to it on the next few pages.

Olivier	Bonjour.
Lynn	Bonjour.
Olivier	Allez-vous à Montpellier?
Lynn	Oui, je vais à Montpellier.
Olivier	Ah, moi aussi. Je suis Olivier.
Lynn	Enchantée. Je suis Lynn.
Olivier	Êtes-vous anglaise?
Lynn	Non, je suis écossaise. Je suis de Glasgow.
Olivier	Ah, vous êtes de Glasgow.
Lynn	Êtes-vous de Montpellier?
Olivier	Non, je suis de Toulouse, mais je vais à Montpellier.
Lynn	Êtes-vous de Montpellier?
Patrick	Oui, je suis de Montpellier.
Olivier	Êtes-vous étudiante?
Lynn	Oui, je suis étudiante en français et en espagnol.
Olivier	Allez-vous à Montpellier pour pratiquer le français?
Lynn	Oui, pour un cours de langue.
Olivier	Ah très bien! Bon, je vais au café.
Lynn	D'accord. À plus tard.
Olivier	À plus tard.

Greetings and other useful words

salut, bonjour	hi, good morning/afternoon
enchanté(e)	pleased to meet you
pour un cours de langue	on a language course
très bien	fine/very well
moi aussi	so am I/me too
bon ...	well ...
d'accord	OK
À plus tard.	See you later.

Verbs

allez-vous à ...?	are you going to ...?
je vais à ...	I'm going to ...
je suis ...	I am ...
êtes-vous ...?	are you ...?
pratiquer	to practise
je travaille	I work

Some nationalities

anglais/anglaise	English m/f
écossais/écossaise	Scottish m/f
espagnol/espagnole	Spanish m/f
français/française	French m/f

A few jobs/occupations

professeur	teacher
artiste	artist
étudiant/étudiante	student m/f

In this section we explain some of the words and expressions introduced in the dialogue.

le café/**la** table	'the café/the table'. To say 'the' in French, we use the word **le** for a noun that is masculine, and **la** for feminine. All nouns in French are considered either masculine or feminine.
Êtes-vous anglaise/de Montpellier/étudiante?	'Are you English/from Montpellier/a student?'
Je suis écossaise/de Toulouse/étudiante.	'I'm Scottish/from Toulouse/a student'. **je suis** (I am) and **vous êtes** (you are) are both parts of the verb **être** (to be).
	You can also see that 'I'm a student' is just **je suis étudiante**. You don't say 'a' before a job or occupation in French.
anglais/anglais**e** espagnol/espagnol**e** français/français**e**	Notice that nationalities are spelt with a small letter, and that their endings vary depending on whether the person is male or female.
Allez-vous à Montpellier?	'Are you going to Montpellier?'
Je vais à Montpellier.	'I'm going to Montpellier.' **Je vais** ('I'm going') and **vous allez** ('you're going') are both parts of the verb **aller** ('to go').

🗹 Your turn 1

Look again at the dialogue. Are the following statements true or false? The answers to the activities in this book are available online at www.collinslanguage.com/click. ⊙ 1

1. They are travelling to Clermont-Ferrand. ....
2. Lynn is English. ....
3. Olivier works in Montpellier. ....

Check your understanding of the dialogue by answering these questions:

1. What does Lynn study? ....
2. Where is Olivier going at the end of the conversation? ....

Find expressions in the dialogue to convey the following: ⊙ 1

1. good morning
2. pleased to meet you
3. me too
4. Are you going to Montpellier?
5. Yes, I'm going to Montpellier.
6. Are you a student?
7. Yes, I'm a student of French and Spanish.
8. see you later

Pronunciation Tips

French pronunciation of consonants is generally similar to English. Where there are difficulties, we'll give you guidance in the Pronunciation Tip section in each unit.

je suis de Toulouse

In French **ui** is pronounced like 'wi' in the English 'Swiss'.

espagnol

In French **gn** is pronounced rather like the 'ni' in the English 'onion'. We'll do some more practice of this sound later.

Ask a female the following questions. Check your answers by ⊙ 2
listening to the audio track.

1. Are you Spanish?   2. Are you English?

Say the following in French (as a man): ⊙ 2

1. I am French.   3. I am a student.
2. I am from Montpellier.

Listen to track 3 and see how much you can understand. Check ⊙ 3
your understanding by answering these questions:

1. What is the man's name? ....
2. Where is he from? ....
3. What is Annie's nationality? ....
4. What is her job? ....

Match the French expressions on the left with their meanings on the right:

1. Je suis australien/australienne.   Are you Irish? *m/f*

2. Êtes-vous irlandais/irlandaise?   I'm a student of Italian.

3. Je vais au café.   I'm Australian. *m/f*

4. Je suis étudiant en italien.   I'm going to the café.

 ## Listen up 2

Listen to Eric and Béatrice talking
about themselves – their work and
their studies. Further information and
exercises based on the text will follow
on the next few pages.

⊙ 4

Eric	Bonsoir. Je suis Eric. Je suis français, de Limoges, mais j'habite et je travaille à Lyon. Je suis professeur de maths. Je suis aussi étudiant en photographie. Maintenant, je vais en cours de photo. Après, je vais au restaurant avec des amis du cours.
Béatrice	Bonsoir, je suis Béatrice. Je suis française, je suis de Rennes, mais j'habite à Paris. Je ne travaille pas. Je suis étudiante en histoire. Maintenant, je vais en cours. Après, je vais au café avec mon copain.

Words and phrases 2

bonsoir	good evening
j'habite	I live
professeur de maths	maths teacher
photographie *f*	photography
cours *m*	class
maintenant	now
après	later on/then
je ne travaille pas	I don't work
histoire *f*	history
copain/copine	boyfriend/girlfriend

j'habite et je travaille | 'I live and I work'. Many verbs saying what I do ('I study', 'I live', etc.) end in –e in French. Unfortunately, both **je suis** and **je vais** are exceptions!

un café/**une** photo | Notice that the word for 'a' can be **un** or **une**. This depends on whether the noun it goes with is considered masculine (**un café**) or feminine (**une photo**). **Un/une** can also mean 'one' – see below.

Numbers

Learning the numbers allows you to do all sorts of things like understand prices, tell the time and even ask someone what bus to catch. Here are the numbers 1 to 12. We'll learn some more later on.

1	un (*when it stands alone*)	**6**	six
	un bar (*when it's with a masculine noun*)	**7**	sept
	une photo – (*when it's with a feminine noun*)	**8**	huit
2	deux	**9**	neuf
3	trois	**10**	dix
4	quatre	**11**	onze
5	cinq	**12**	douze

Your turn 2

Now, using the vocabulary that you have learned so far (and without using the transcript on the previous page!) listen to the dialogue again and fill in the gaps to check you've understood the descriptions. You can check your answers at www.collinslanguage.com/click.   ◉ 4

1. Bonsoir. .... Eric. Je suis ...., de Limoges, mais j'habite et je travaille à .... Je suis professeur de maths. Je suis aussi .... en photographie. Maintenant, ... en cours de photo. Après, ... au restaurant avec des amis du ....

2. ...., je suis Béatrice. Je suis ...., je suis de Rennes, mais j'habite à .... Je ne travaille pas. .... étudiante en histoire. Maintenant, ... en cours. Après, ... au café avec mon copain.

Rewrite the following anagrams to create French numbers:

1. THIU	4. RAQETU	7. SIROT	10. FUNE	13. NICQ
....	....	....	....	....

2. XDI	5. ZEDUO	8. ENU	11. UXED
....	....	....	....

3. NU	6. TSEP	9. XSI	12. ZONE
....	....	....	....

· ·

Say the following in French. Check your answers by listening to the audio track: ⊙ 5

1. hello
2. I am English. *(try both male and female)*
3. I live in Lyon.
4. I am a student. *(as a woman)*

· ·

Listen and understand. In which order are the numbers 1–12 ⊙ 6
pronounced? Mark the order against the list of French numbers below:

un	cinq	neuf ...1............
deux ..2............	six	dix ....
trois	sept	onze ....
quatre	huit	douze ....

· ·

There are two mistakes in the following text. Can you spot them?

Bonjour. Je suis Marjorie. Je suis français. J'habite à Toulouse, mais je suis Bordeaux. Je suis économiste.

Here's an opportunity for you to revise the language you've learned in this unit.

Supply the correct option in each case:

1. .... vous française?

   a. Suis   b. Allez   c. Êtes

2. Non, je ne .... pas française.

   a. allez   b. suis   c. vais

3. .... vous à Montpellier?

   a. Vais   b. Suis   c. Allez

4. Oui, je .... à Montpellier.

   a. êtes   b. vais   c. allez

• •

Write the numbers 1–12 in French. We've started you off:

1.	un	7.	....
2.	deux	8.	....
3.	....	9.	....
4.	....	10.	....
5.	....	11.	....
6.	....	12.	....

Où est ...?
Where is ...?

2

You'll learn how to find your way around using public transport, and to locate places you need to find. We'll also study how to say what time things happen.

Traveller's tip

Public transport in France is efficient and good value for money. Major cities, such as Lyon, Bordeaux or Montpellier, have introduced or brought back tram routes in their city centres. Integrated transport networks, offering interconnected subway, bus and tram services, allow visitors to get around without having to worry about traffic jams, finding a parking space or getting change for the parking meter.

The main rule when travelling on French public transport is not to forget to stamp your ticket otherwise it will not be valid! In big cities a single ticket will usually allow you to combine travel by tram, bus and **métro** train to reach your destination. Further savings can be made by buying a ten-trip ticket – **un ticket 10 voyages** giving you, say, ten journeys for the price of eight. You can also buy a pass – check out the **ParisVisite** pass for example. If you are a night owl you could also take the

Noctilien, a night bus service in the Paris area.

Travelling between cities by train is a delight in modern, fast, punctual and comfortable trains. The national rail network, **SNCF**, has a number of inter-city jewels in its crown, notably the high-speed **TGV** lines between Lille and Paris, Paris and Marseille, or even Lille and Avignon and in the west, linking cities like Bordeaux, Biarritz, Toulouse and Perpignan.

Air France also offers many destinations within France.

dix-sept 17

In the last unit we met masculine and feminine words. Now we're going to use **il** and **elle** to say 'it' depending on whether the word is masculine or feminine in French. We'll also learn the language you need to say what time a bus or train leaves and arrives.

À quelle heure ...? At what time ...?
Où est ...? Where is ...?

 ## Listen up 1

We've arrived in France and are outside the airport looking   ⦿ 7
to continue our journey to our destination. Listen to the
sequence of short dialogues as many times as you need.

First, we need to ask where the bus stop is:

Tourist	Excusez-moi.
Passer-by	Oui?
Tourist	Où est l'arrêt de bus?
Passer-by	Il est là-bas, à gauche.
Tourist	Ah d'accord, merci.
Passer-by	De rien.

Now we're in the city centre looking for the underground station.   ⦿ 8
Another passer-by is telling us that it's in the main street:

Tourist	S'il vous plaît, où est la station de métro?
Passer-by	Elle est dans la rue principale.
Tourist	Merci beaucoup.
Passer-by	De rien.

Now we need to buy a ticket – just a one-way ticket for the first journey. You'll hear the expression for 'one-way', as well as the price (listen carefully for this – there's a question about it later!):

Tourist	Un aller simple, s'il vous plaît.
Clerk	Deux euros.
Tourist	Merci.

Now we're going on a day trip to Versailles, a royal palace south-west of Paris, but this time we need a return ticket:

Tourist	Je vais à Versailles, un aller-retour, s'il vous plaît. Combien ça coûte?
Clerk	Douze euros, s'il vous plaît.
Tourist	Merci beaucoup.
Clerk	De rien. Au revoir.
Tourist	Au revoir.

🔊 Words and phrases 1

Où est …? Il/Elle est …	Where is …? It's …
l'arrêt de bus	the bus stop
là-bas/ici	there/here
à gauche/à droite	on the left/on the right
d'accord	okay
merci (beaucoup)	thank you (very much)
s'il vous plaît	please
la station de métro	the underground station
la rue principale	the main street
de rien	you're welcome/not at all
un aller simple	a single ticket
un aller-retour	a return (ticket)
Combien ça coûte?	How much is it?
au revoir	goodbye

One of the confusing things about French is that all the words are either masculine or feminine – even the underground station and the bus stop. So when you are talking about them you have to choose between **il** or **elle** to mean 'it':

Où est l'arrêt de bus?	'Where's the bus stop?'
Il est là-bas.	It's there.'
Où est la station de métro?	'Where the underground station?'
Elle est dans la rue principale.	'It's in the main street.'

You'll have noticed the accent on the word **où**. There are various rules determining why a word has an accent; in this case, it helps us tell the difference between two words: **où** which means 'where' and **ou** which means 'or'. Both are pronounced in exactly the same way.

The accent on the **é** in **métro** tells you to pronounce it like the English 'ay'. You will see how other accents affect pronunciation as you go through the units.

You'll also have noticed **ça** (pronounced *sah*) in '**Combien ça coûte**?' In French, shoppers ask 'How much is **that**?'

 Your turn 1

Listen again to the dialogues. Are the following statements true or false? The answers to the activities in this book are available online at www.collinslanguage.com/click.

⊙ 9 & 10

1. The single ticket was 3 euros. . . . .

2. The return to Versailles was 12 euros. . . . .

. . . .

Match the photos with the French word for each form of transport:

1. le bus

2. le métro

3. le taxi

4. le train

a.

b.

c.

d.

Find expressions in the dialogues to convey the following: ⊙ 7, 8 & 10

1. Where is the bus stop? ....

2. Where is the underground station? ....

3. How much is it? ....

4. It's twelve euros. ....

. . . .

Make sure you can also say the following:

1. hello

2. please

3. thanks

4. thank you very much

5. not at all

6. goodbye

Pronunciation Tips

station
The **t** in **tion** is pronounced *ss* in French.

principale, rien, simple, combien
in, **im** and **ien** are pronounced the same way. It's as if you wanted to say 'an' with a blocked nose. The 'n' or 'm' are not really pronounced, they just tell you to say this sound 'through your nose'.

au revoir, beaucoup
au and **eau** are pronounced like 'oh'. Think of 'beau'!

beaucoup, euros, plaît, est
You might have noticed that French does not pronounce last consonants very often!

. . . .

Ask for the following tickets in French. Check your answers by listening to the audio track. ⊙ 11

1. A return to Lyon, please.

2. A single ticket, please.

Now try and remember how to ask these two questions. Again, listen to the audio track to check your answers. 12

1. Where is the bus stop?
2. How much is it?

Listen to the dialogue on track 13 and then answer these questions: ● 13

1. Where does the person want to go? ....
2. What sort of ticket do they ask for? ....
3. How much does it cost? ....

Rearrange the word order in these expressions so that they make sense:

1. s'il aller vous simple un plaît ....
2. station est métro la où de? ....
3. euros dix coûte ça ....
4. principale la dans rue c'est ....

Listen up 2

Now we're at the bus station. The passenger wants to get a bus to the capital. We're told what time it leaves and what time it arrives. Listen out for the patterns of how times are expressed: ● 14

Passenger	À quelle heure part le bus?
Driver	Il part à quatre heures et demie.
Passenger	Et à quelle heure arrive-t-il à Paris?
Driver	Il arrive à six heures moins le quart environ.
Passenger	Merci beaucoup.

Making enquiries at the railway station: the customer wants to go to Orly airport. This time, you'll hear not only its departure and arrival times, but also the price of the ticket: ⊙ 15

Customer	Bonjour.
Clerk	Bonjour.
Customer	À quelle heure part le train pour l'aéroport d'Orly?
Clerk	Il part à dix heures.
Customer	Et à quelle heure arrive-t-il à l'aéroport?
Clerk	Il arrive à l'aéroport à onze heures cinq.
Customer	Combien ça coûte?
Clerk	Six euros pour un aller simple, et onze pour un aller-retour.
Customer	Très bien. Merci.
Clerk	De rien.

🔊 Words and phrases 2

le train	the train
À quelle heure part ...?	(At) What time does ... leave?
Il part à ...	It leaves/departs at ...
À quelle heure arrive ...?	(At) What time does ... arrive?
Il arrive à ...	It arrives at ...
environ	about

🔒 Unlocking the language 2

À quelle heure?   The basic question really asks 'at what hour?' Then you can add a verb:

À quelle heure arrive ...?   'At what time does ... arrive?'
Il arrive à onze heures.   It arrives at eleven o'clock.

Notice that the verb is the same in the question and the answer.

à une heure   at one o'clock
à deux heures   at two o'clock
à trois heures   at three o'clock

Notice that the **heure** at 1.00 becomes **heures** from 2.00 to 12.00.

Telling the time

Here's how to say some more complex times:

at 11.**05**	à onze heures **cinq**
at 11.**10**	à onze heures **dix**
at 11.**15**	à onze heures **et quart**
at 11.**30**	à onze heures **et demie**
at 11.**45**	à midi **moins le quart**
at 11.**50**	à midi **moins dix**
at 11.**55**	à midi **moins cinq**

So **et** means 'past' with 'quarter' and 'half', and **moins** equates to minutes 'to' the next hour.

↗ Your turn 2

Match up the clock faces with the times:

1. cinq heures et quart

2. sept heures moins le quart

3. onze heures dix

4. neuf heures

a.   b.   c.   d.

· ·

Write the following in full in French:

1. at 4.10 ....

2. at 6.15 ....

3. at 9.30 ....

4. at 10.45 ....

5. at 12.55 *(be careful!)* ....

· ·

Can you say the following in French? Check your answers by listening to the audio track. 16

1. The train leaves at three o'clock.

2. The bus arrives at ten o'clock.

Listen to the dialogue. Try and answer these three questions: 🔘 17

1. Where is the passenger going? ....

2. What time does the train (*here*, **le TGV**) leave? ....

3. What time does it get to its destination? ....

. . . .

Answer the following questions in French, using the prompts in brackets:

1. Où est la station de métro? (main street)

2. Combien coûte un aller simple? (4 euros)

3. À quelle heure part le train? (9.15)

4. À quelle heure arrive le bus? (9.50)

🔄 Let's recap

Here's an opportunity for you to revise the language you've learned in this unit.

Use one of the following words to fill each of the gaps below:

part	dans	le	arrive	à	est
heure	combien	quart	aller	où	

1. .... l'arrêt de bus?

2. .... quelle heure .... le train pour Paris?

3. Il part à deux heures moins le ....

4. À quelle heure .... le train à Paris?

5. À quelle .... part .... bus?

6. .... coûte un ....-retour?

7. C'est .... la rue principale.

Un peu d'aide 3
A bit of help

We'll put together an essential survival kit to cover any situations in which you might run into problems, from simply not understanding to more complex situations such as health issues and loss of possessions.

Traveller's tip

Among the problems expressed by students of French are the notions that French people talk much more quickly than speakers of English, and that regional accents can be hard to follow. It's a fact that accents from the south of France tend to be more difficult to understand, as people speak faster and pronounce sounds differently. The speed issue may or may not be true, but it's inevitable that there will be times when you don't catch what's been said to you, so we're going to focus on a few expressions to make it clear that you haven't understood, to ask for repetitions, and so on.

You may find you've simply taken a wrong turning and can't find your way back to the hotel, or to the particular square or museum you're looking for. It's a good idea to have the basics of asking for (and understanding) directions from A to B.

It's fair to say that France is generally a safe, friendly and easy-going place to spend time, but in any city or country there will always be the minority element looking to pick your pocket or trick you in some way. We'll show you what you need to say if you've lost your passport, money, etc.

Equally, there's no legislating for when illness can strike, at home or abroad. We'll equip you with the basic language necessary to explain what's happened so that you can get the correct treatment.

In this unit, as well as focusing on situation-specific language, we'll dip briefly into the past tense to say what has happened. This is a one-off – the rest of the course returns to primarily present-tense language.

J'ai perdu mon passeport.	I've lost my passport.
On m'a volé mon portefeuille.	Someone has stolen my wallet.

We'll also have a look at the verb **pouvoir** ('to be able to') to ask questions like 'Can you help me?'

Pouvez-vous m'aider ?	Can you help me?

 ## Listen up 1

Listen to the series of short expressions on the audio track covering problems of understanding. You'll have the opportunity to practise them in a couple of pages. ◎ 18

What if you get lost? Listen to the set of useful expressions. ◎ 19

From now on, the dialogues will not appear here in the book but you can access all of the CD transcripts at any time online at www.collinslanguage.com/click.

Words and phrases 1

Pardon?	Pardon? (not having heard)
Pouvez-vous répéter, s'il vous plaît?	Can you repeat, please?
plus lentement	more slowly
Je ne comprends pas.	I don't understand.
Je ne parle pas français.	I don't speak French.
Parlez-vous anglais?	Do you speak English?
Je suis étranger/étrangère.	I'm a foreigner. m/f
Je ne suis pas d'ici.	I'm not from here.

Pouvez-vous me l'écrire, s'il vous plaît?	Can you write it down for me, please?
Excusez-moi/Pardon	Sorry (excuse me)
Pouvez-vous m'aider?	Can you help me?
je suis perdu/perdue	I'm lost *m/f*
Où est la place principale?	Where's the main square?
Où est l'Hôtel du Centre?	Where's the Hotel du Centre?
Où sont les toilettes?	Where are the toilets?
Dans quelle direction est la gare	Which way to the railway station?
Pouvez-vous m'indiquer où je suis sur la carte?	Can you show me on the map where I am?

Unlocking the language 1

Je **ne** comprends **pas**. Notice that in order to make any verb negative, you
Je **ne** parle **pas** français. surround it with **ne** and **pas**.
Je **ne** suis **pas** d'ici.

Pouvez-vous m'aider? **Pouvez** ('you can' or 'can you?') is part of the verb **pouvoir**
Pouvez-vous répéter? ('to be able') and is very useful for asking if someone **can**
Pouvez-vous me l'écrire? do something. For the next verb, like 'help', 'repeat', just
use the infinitive form as you find it in the dictionary – you
don't need to do any work to it!

pardon As well as the general **pardon**, there are two ways of
saying sorry that can be used both for attracting attention
and for apologising.

Pardon
Excusez-moi
Je suis désolé(e) (*only for apologising*)

The French alphabet

a	(ah)	**p**	(pay)
b	(bay)	**q**	(kew, *same pronunciation as 'u' preceded by 'k'*)
c	(say)		
d	(day)	**r**	(air)
e	(uh)	**s**	(ess)
f	(ef)	**t**	(tay)
g	(zhay: *'zh' sounds like the 's' in leisure*)	**u**	(ew, *put your lips as if to say 'oo' but say 'ee'*)
h	(ash)		
i	(ee, *like the beginning of the English 'even'*)	**v**	(vay)
j	(zhee: *'zh' sounds like the 's' in leisure*)	**w**	(doo-bluh vay)
k	(kah)	**x**	(iks)
l	(el)	**y**	(ee-grek, *literally 'Greek letter i'*)
m	(emm)		
n	(enn)	**z**	(zed)
o	(oh)		

It would be useful at this point to study carefully the letters needed to spell your name and the street and town where you live. Practise spelling these out until you can do it without looking at the guide.

↗ Your turn 1

Spend a few minutes rereading Words and phrases 1, then see if you can remember expressions to convey the following. The answers to the activities in this book are available online at www.collinslanguage.com/click

1. I don't understand.

2. Can you repeat, please?

3. More slowly.

4. I'm not from here.

5. Can you write it down for me, please?

6. Can you help me?

Pronunciation Tips

anglais, français, aide, plaît

ai sounds like 'Eh!' in English.

anglais, français, étranger, centre

Another 'nosey' sound: **an** and **en** sound the same and you have to say this in your nose again, without pronouncing the 'n'. It's a bit like the sound *ahn* but without the *n*.

How would you say the following in French? Check your answers by listening to the audio track. 21

1. I'm lost (*spoken by a man*)

2. I'm lost (*spoken by a woman*)

3. I'm foreign (*spoken by a man*)

4. I'm foreign (*spoken by a woman*)

Listen to the people talking and make sure you have understood the problems they're describing: 22

1. Where does the first person want to go?

2. Where is the second speaker from?

Match the predicaments on the left with the English translations on the right:

1. Je ne parle pas français.   I'm a foreigner.

2. Je suis étranger.   I'm lost.

3. Je ne comprends pas.   I'm not from here.

4. Je suis perdu.   I don't speak French.

5. Je ne suis pas d'ici.   I don't understand.

Au commissariat de police/At the police station: ⊚ 2 3

Listen to the dialogue between a tourist and a police officer. The explanatory sections will help with any words you can't pick out first time.

À l'hôpital (aux urgences)/At the hospital (Accident and Emergency): ⊚ 2 4

Now listen to a tourist explaining his health condition at the A & E reception desk.

Remember that you can see a written version of all of the audio tracks by going online to www.collinslanguage.com/click.

Words and phrases 2

De quoi s'agit-il?	What's the problem? (lit. 'What is it about?')
On m'a volé mon portefeuille.	I've had my wallet stolen (lit. 'Someone has stolen my wallet.')
quand?	when?
ce matin	this morning
Vous n'avez vu personne?	You didn't see anyone?
J'ai perdu ...	I've lost ...
argent *m*	money
clé *f*	key
Ne vous inquiétez pas.	Don't worry.

consulat *m*	consulate
je vous en prie	not at all – more formal than **de rien**
remplissez ce formulaire	fill out this form
prénom *m*	first name
nom *m*	surname
domicile *m*	home address
nationalité *f*	nationality
Mon bras est enflé.	My arm is swollen.
Avez-vous mal?/J'ai mal.	Does it hurt (you)?/It hurts (me).
appeler	to call
médecin *m/f*	doctor
être en vacances	to be on holiday
carte *f* d'assurance maladie	health insurance card – if you are an EU citizen, get hold of a European Health Insurance Card before you travel to France: it entitles you to the same treatment as the residents of the country you are visiting.
asseyez-vous	sit down

 ## Unlocking the language 2

On m'a volé …	'Someone has stolen …' **On** has various meanings, but in this case, it means 'someone'.
J'ai perdu …	'I've lost …' This is another past tense – again, just focus on the meaning rather than how it's formed. You can start your explanation with **j'ai perdu …**, then list any items lost.
remplir	**Remplir** is the verb 'to complete/fill out (a form)'. The speaker here is using a polite command form, as the two people do not know each other well.
Avez-vous mal (à …)? J'ai mal (à …)	**Mal** is from the same family as **maladie** ('disease'). What is being said here is 'Have you pain (in …)?' and 'I have pain (in …)'. If it's needed, the painful body part comes after the **à** (for feminine words), **au** (for masculine words) or **aux** (for plural words) in both question and statement.

Match the photos with the French words. You don't know all of these words yet but can you work them out?

1. les clés
2. l'argent
3. la carte bancaire
4. le portable
5. le passeport
6. le portefeuille

a.

b.

c.

d.

e.

f.

. . . .

Find expressions in the dialogues (tracks 23 and 24) to convey the following: 🔊 23 & 24

1. Can you help me, please?
2. I've had my wallet stolen.
3. I've lost my passport.
4. My arm is swollen.
5. It hurts.

. . . .

Can you say the following in French? The language from the dialogue is rearranged slightly. Check your answers by listening to the audio track. 🔊 25

1. I've had my passport stolen.
2. I've lost my wallet.
3. This morning at ten o'clock in the main square.

. . . .

Listen to track 26. Make sure you've understood what is being said in these expressions. 🔊 26

1. What has been lost in the first instance? ....
2. What's the problem in the second situation? ....

Here are some other body parts that might be hurting you. See if you can match them up: we haven't learned them yet, so you'll need to guess! If you can't guess, use the free dictionary at www.collinslanguage.com.

1.	... à la tête	my tooth
2.	... à la dent	my stomach
3.	... au pied	my head
4.	... à l'estomac	my leg
5.	... à la jambe	my foot

Let's recap

In this unit we've set out a couple of usages of a past tense. There's no need to learn the tense, but the expressions themselves are handy to keep in mind. Here's a reminder:

On m'a volé ...   Someone has stolen my ...

J'ai perdu ...   I've lost ...

....

The following sentences have their words in the wrong order. Can you rectify them?

1. m'aider vous s'il pouvez plaît vous? ....
2. où pouvez la sur vous m'indiquer suis carte je? ....
3. portefeuille volé mon on m'a. ....
4. très bras au j'ai mal. ....

....

Choose the correct option to complete each sentence:

1. Donnez-moi .... passeport, s'il vous plaît.

   a. de   **b.** la   **c.** votre   **d.** une

2. Où .... l'Hôtel du Centre?

   a. est   **b.** suis   **c.** avez   **d.** ai

3. Remplissez .... formulaire.

   a. cet   **b.** ce   **c.** ces   **d.** cette

4. Avez-vous très .... ?

   a. bras   **b.** mal   **c.** j'ai   **d.** problème

À l'hôtel
At the hotel

We'll cover the language you'll need to check into a hotel in France and discover what facilities it has to offer. We'll also be taking a look at some of the different types of places to stay in France.

Traveller's tip

Every year, millions of us head to France seeking sunshine, good food and drink, culture or the charm of Paris.

Most hotel and tourism staff speak some English. However, there's a real achievement in speaking some French on holiday, and French people will be delighted you've made an effort to learn their language.

Our first experience of a French hotel is usually on the coasts or in Paris as part of a package holiday. But next time, you may want to do things more independently. Here are some of the key words in considering accommodation.

Backpackers should look out for **une auberge de jeunesse**, 'youth hostel'. Expect a multicultural environment and a lively time, for a very reasonable price.

Campsites – **campings** – are very popular too, from basic ones lost in remote and beautiful places, to 5-star sites with all the facilities

and attractions a family could ask for.

Un hôtel is indeed a hotel. Expect a higher level of service (and price!), usually with en-suite facilities, air-conditioning, etc. Credit cards are widely accepted, and most French hotels take bookings online.

For a taste of local life, try the **chambres d'hôtes**, the equivalent of B&Bs. However, some also offer a **table d'hôte** where you can join your host for dinner – a nice way to try the local cuisine and chat with French people.

In this unit, we'll mainly be revising two structures we met earlier. They're both very useful for finding your way around and planning your time.

Où sont ...?   Where are ...? (This time we're asking about plural things)

À quelle heure ...?   At what time is ...?

Listen up 1

A couple arrive at a French hotel and check in. Listen to the dialogue and see if you can pick out the various stages of the process.

⊙ 27

Transcripts for all of the audio tracks on the CD are available online at www.collinslanguage.com/click.

Words and phrases 1

Nous avons une réservation.		We have a reservation.
une chambre	pour une personne	a single room
	pour deux personnes	a double room
	avec un lit double	a room with a double bed
	avec deux lits simples	a room with two beds (i.e. a twin room)
	avec salle de bains	a room with an en-suite bathroom
	avec douche	a room with a shower
pour dix nuits		for ten nights. When you're booking something **for** a period of time, remember to use **pour** (+ **deux heures, trois jours, sept nuits,** etc.)

carte *f* bancaire	bank card
étage *m* – au quatrième étage	storey/floor – on the fourth floor
rez-de-chaussée *m* – au rez-de-chaussée	ground floor – on the ground floor
petit-déjeuner *m*/prendre le petit-déjeuner	breakfast/to have breakfast
ce soir	tonight
Nous prenons l'apéritif avec des amis.	We're having an aperitif with some friends.
autre chose	something else/anything else

 ## Unlocking the language 1

voilà	'Here you are.' This is the response to **Pouvez-vous me donner ...?** above.
Où est ...? Il est .../**Elle est** ...	'Where is ...?' '**It's** (located) ...' When speaking about places, remember that words are either masculine or feminine and so 'it' is either **il** or **elle**.
il est à gauche/droite	'it's on the left/the right'
tout droit	'straight ahead'
Pouvez-vous me donner ...?	'Can you give me ...?'
de six heures **à** neuf heures	From six o'clock to nine o'clock. Remember the little construction **de ... à** 'from ... to' - it's very useful.

Your turn 1

Check your understanding of the dialogue by answering these questions. The answers to the activities are all available online at www.collinslanguage.com/click.

1. How many nights will the couple be staying? ....

2. What is the room number? ....

3. What time is breakfast? ....

4. What time is dinner? ....

Numbers 13–29

In unit 1, we looked at the numbers from 1 to 12. Here's the next batch, from 13 to 29.

13 treize	**15** quinze
14 quatorze	**16** seize

Notice the structure of the next few: e.g. 18 is literally 'ten-eight'.

17 dix-sept	**19** dix-neuf
18 dix-huit	**20** vingt

21 breaks down as 'twenty and one'.
Then the numbers from 22 to 29 follow the same structure as in English.

21 vingt et un	**26** vingt-six
22 vingt-deux	**27** vingt-sept
23 vingt-trois	**28** vingt-huit
24 vingt-quatre	**29** vingt-neuf
25 vingt-cinq	

Numbers 30–99

Now let's look at higher numbers from 30 to 99. In the same style as the 20s, all the numbers ending in 1 from 31 to 91 (except 81) include 'et'. For all the others 'et' is dropped and a hyphen is used instead. In France, 70 is 'sixty-ten', 80 is 'four twenties'(a bit like 'four score') and 90 is 'four times twenty-ten'. In Belgium and Switzerland you may hear other ways of saying these numbers.

30 trente	**46** quarante-six
31 trente et un	**50** cinquante
32 trente-deux	**60** soixante
40 quarante	**70** soixante-dix

From 70 to 79, the numbers are made up of 60 plus 'the teens', e.g. 75 is soixante-quinze (60 + 15).

80 quatre-vingts

The **s** is silent in **vingts**. Notice that after 80, the **s** disappears, e.g. 87 is **quatre-vingt-sept.**

90 quatre-vingt-dix   **99** quatre-vingt-dix-neuf

Be careful with the similarity between 60 and 70, and between 80 and 90.

Find expressions in the dialogue to convey the following: ⊙ 27

1. We have a room booked.

2. For ten nights.

3. Your passport and your bank card.

4. On the ground floor.

5. Dinner is served from seven until nine o'clock in the evening.

6. Is there anything else you need?

7. See you later.

Pronunciation Tips

neuf, heures

the sound **eu** is pronounced like *uh*, like the vowel sounds in 'earn' and 'bird'. Later in this unit, you'll come across **bœuf**: the tied **o** and **e + u** sound like **eu** too.

bonsoir, non

another 'nosey' sound. Once again you don't pronounce the **n**, You say it through your nose.

quatrième

In French, the **u** after a **q** is not pronounced. You just say *ka* for 'quatrième'.

⋯⋯⋯⋯⋯⋯⋯⋯⋯⋯⋯⋯⋯⋯⋯⋯

Now, using the language you've learned in this unit, think about ⊙ 28
arriving at a hotel, but this time with slightly different requirements.
How would you say the following? Check your answers by listening to
the audio track.

1. A single room with a shower.

2. A double room with an en-suite bathroom.

3. A twin room.

4. A room with a double bed.

5. A room for fourteen nights.

⋯⋯⋯⋯⋯⋯⋯⋯⋯⋯⋯⋯⋯⋯⋯⋯

Listen to the guests and make sure you have understood their ⊙ 29
requirements:

1. What sort of room does the first man mention? ....

2. How many nights will the woman be staying? ....

3. What bathroom facility is requested by the second man? ....

Match the questions on the left with the answers on the right:

1. Pouvez-vous me donner votre passeport, s'il vous plaît?

   Il est de six heures à huit heures et demie.

2. Où est l'ascenseur?

   Non, merci.

3. À quelle heure est le petit-déjeuner?

   Il est là, à gauche.

4. Autre chose?

   Oui, voilà.

· ·

Write out the following numbers in full:

1. 32 ....
2. 44 ....
3. 59 ....
4. 60 ....

5. 67 ....
6. 76 ....
7. 81 ....
8. 93 ....

 ## Listen up 2

Later the same day, Linda returns to the hotel reception desk for some advice. Listen to the dialogue and see how much you can understand. You can refer to the transcript online at www.collinslanguage.com/click if you need to.

◎ 30

Words and phrases 2

renseigner	to give information
bien sûr	of course
manger	to eat
par exemple	for example
à pied	on foot
au bout de	at the end of
Ne vous inquiétez pas!	Don't worry!
il ferme	it closes
tard	late

Tout va bien?	This is a very handy little question, which can be used to enquire about someone's health, how things are going or how they are getting on with a specific task or activity: the English 'how's it going?' is possibly the nearest equivalent.
Où sont …?	'Where are …?' **Ils sont** means 'they are'. We can now contrast **Où est la station de métro?** ('Where is the underground station?') with **Où sont les restaurants?** ('Where are the restaurants?')
à cinq mètres / à dix minutes	To say how far away something is (either in distance or in time) the little word **à** – it equates to the notion of 'away' in English: **C'est à dix kilomètres/minutes** ('It's ten kilometres/minutes away')
À quelle heure est le dîner? / Il est à huit heures.	When you're asking what time something is or happens, remember to begin the question with **à** ('at').
C'est loin/près d'ici.	'It's far away/close by.'
Ne vous inquiétez pas.	'Don't worry.' This is quite a complex structure in French, but we can just learn it here as a one-off.

Your turn 3

Check your understanding of what you heard in the dialogue by answering these questions: ⊚ 30

1. What is Linda looking for? ……………………………………

2. How far is it? ……………………………………

3. Where is it exactly? ……………………………………

4. When does it close? ……………………………………

Can you say the following in French? Check your answers by listening to the audio track.   ⊚ 31

1. Is it far from here?

2. It's ten minutes away on foot.

3. Could you give me some information?

Make sure you can understand what is being said in these short dialogues. Listen out in particular for the following information:

1. Where is the hotel, and how many minutes does it take to get there? ....

....

2. Is the lift on the left or the right? How many metres away is it? ....

....

Looking at the map above, complete these directions:

● S'il vous plaît, où est le restaurant?

● Le restaurant .... au .... de la .... principale, à

  ....

The following dialogue has one mistake in each line. Use the language you've learned above to work out what's wrong:

Tourist	Bonsoir. Où sont le restaurant?
Receptionist	La restaurant est rue du Bœuf.
Tourist	Merci beaucoup. C'est loin ici?
Receptionist	Non, c'est à bout de la rue, à gauche.
Tourist	Très bon. À plus tard.
Receptionist	Bon soirée.

Study the following short dialogues based around what time events begin. They're just here for you to read, recognise and use for practice.

1. À quelle heure **est** le dîner?

   Il **est** de sept heures à neuf heures.

2. **Nous mangeons** à quelle heure?

   Nous mangeons à huit heures.

3. À quelle heure **ferme** le restaurant?

   Il ferme à une heure du matin.

Useful Tips

- Notice that the verb in the question is reused in the answer.
- Remember the usage of **à** in both the question and the answer.

Choose the correct option to complete each sentence:

1. Bonsoir. Nous avons une ....

   a. chambre   b. hôtel   c. réservation   d. petit-déjeuner

2. Le restaurant est .... gauche.

   a. la   b. de   c. le   d. à

3. À quelle heure est le dîner? C'est à .... heures.

   a. huit   b. une   c. midi   d. soir

4. Où .... l'hôtel?

   a. sont   b. est   c. a   d. suis

L'apéritif
The aperitif

5

We'll be looking at the popular French tradition of having a pre-dinner drink, **un apéritif**, as well as learning how to order drinks in a bar.

We'll be learning and using several useful new verbs in this unit. These are vital for ordering drinks and snacks.

Il y a ...?	Is there/Are there ...?
Je voudrais ...	I would like ...
Je prends ...	I'll take ...

A couple are in a bar, wondering what snacks to have with their
apéritifs. Their waiter tells them more about the options available.
Listen to the conversation, but beware: this section may get your
mouth watering!

⊙ 33

Transcripts for the audio tracks on the CD are available online at
www.collinslanguage.com/click.

Words and phrases 1

Vous désirez?	What would you like?
carte *f*	menu
amuse-bouches *m pl*	appetizers (**bouche** means 'mouth')
Voyons ...	Let's see ...
Qu'est-ce que c'est celui-là?	What's that one?
assiette *f*	plate/dish
jambon *m*	ham
viande *f*	meat
dedans	inside
en fait	actually
végétarien/végétarienne	vegetarian *m/f*
manger	to eat
tartine *f*	slice of bread (sometimes toasted) spread with a topping
sans	without
saumon *m*	salmon
celui-ci *m*/celle-ci *f*	this (one)

celui-là *m*/celle-là *f*	that (one)
ceux-ci *m*/celles-ci *f*	these (ones)
ceux-là *m*/celles-là *f*	those (ones)
fromage *m*, au fromage	cheese, with cheese
légumes *m pl*, aux légumes	vegetables, with vegetables
mini-quiche *f*	snack-sized quiche
mini-pizza *f*	snack-sized pizza
pour moi ...	for me ...
tapenade *f*	a blend of black olives and capers chopped and crushed.
Comme boissons?	(What can I get you) to drink?
verre *m* de vin *m* blanc pétillant	glass of sparkling white wine. **Un verre** is used for all drinks. **blanc** is the word for 'white' (you can remember it from the English 'blank'). You can also order **vin rouge** (red) or **rosé** (rosé), **non-pé** (still) and **pétillant** (sparkling).
maison	house (wine, etc.)
sans alcool	alcohol-free. With alcohol is **alcoolisé(e)**.
Je vous apporte ça tout de suite.	I'll bring you that straight away.

🔒 Unlocking the language 1

Il y a ...(?)	'There is .../There are .../Is there ...?/Are there ...?' **a** is from the verb **avoir** ('to have'), plus **y** ('there'). It is used in a variety of contexts, here to ask whether something is available and to refer to the content of a snack ('Does it contain/Is there ...?'). The plural is the same as the singular.
Je voudrais ...	This is part of the verb **vouloir** ('to want'), and is used here to order something to eat/drink, by saying 'I would like ...'
Je prends ...	I'll take/I'll have ...' This can be used as an alternative to **je voudrais.**
Pour moi ...	Another very straightforward way to order things: 'For me ...'

Match the photos with the *amuse-bouches*. Remember that the answers to all of the activities are available online at www.collinslanguage.com/click.

1. petits-fours
2. mini-pizza
3. tartine de tapenade

a.   b.   c.

Find expressions in the dialogue to convey the following:

1. Is there an appetizers menu?
2. What is that one?
3. I'm vegetarian (*female*).
4. I would like one cheese canapé/toast.
5. Something to drink?
6. I'll have a glass of white wine.

Pronunciation Tips

jambon, viande, mange, blanc, pétillant, en, dans, sans
As we saw earlier, **an** and **en** are pronounced in your nose and you don't really pronounce the 'n'. The 'n' is just a sign that you have to do a nosey sound.

moi, voilà, boisson
oi is pronounced like 'wa' in the English word 'watt'

ça
ça is pronounced *ssa*. The little tail under the **c** is called a cedilla and it's used to 'soften' the 'c'. **ca, co, cu** are pronounced *kah, koh* and *kew*, however **ça** and **ço** are pronounced *sah* and *soh*.

en fait
In this instance, the final **t** is pronounced: *feht*.

Now, using the language you've learned above, think about ordering some different appetizers and drinks. How would you say the following? Begin each order with *je voudrais* ... Check your answers by listening to track 34.

◉ 34

1. three vegetable quiches
2. some snack-sized pizzas
3. two cheese toasts
4. two alcohol-free cocktails
5. a glass of red wine

• •

Listen to the three food and drink orders on track 35 and answer a question on each:

◉ 35

1. How many canapés of each flavour are ordered? ....
2. What is ordered with the quiche? ....
3. Is it two alcohol-free aperitifs and a glass of white wine, or something different?

....

• •

Listen back to the first dialogue in this unit and see if you can identify the following appetizers from their photos:

1. ....
2. ....
3. ....

a.

b.

c.

• •

Match the French expressions on the left with their translations on the right:

1. Il y a de la viande dans ceux-ci?
2. le cocktail maison
3. Je voudrais une quiche au fromage.
4. trois apéritifs

the house cocktail

three aperitifs

Have these got meat in them?

I would like a cheese quiche.

Listen up 2

In the next bar, it's time to order some drinks. You'll hear an order for both hot and cold drinks, as well as some nibbles. See how much you can understand.

⊙ 36

Words and phrases 2

demi *m*	a half pint of beer
Autre chose?	Anything else?
(café) décaféiné	decaffeinated coffee. The main coffee orders in France are **un café/un espresso** (an espresso), **un café crème** (an espresso with a small amount of cream) and **un café filtre** (filter coffee). The nearest thing to white coffee is **un café au lait**.
Il y a quelque chose à grignoter?	Are there any nibbles?
Il y a ...	There are ...
chips *f pl*	crisps
olives *f pl*	olives
cacahuètes *f pl*	peanuts
biscuits apéritif *m pl*	small savoury biscuits

Unlocking the language 2

suis   'I am' from **être** ('to be'). You learned this in Unit 1. Can you remember some other phrases you have learned using 'I am'?

allergique   allergic

Find the appetizers and drinks hidden in these anagrams:

1. athècuaces ....
2. idem ....
3. vesilo ....
4. vni ....
5. tinerat ....
6. forgema ....
7. afcé ....
8. uchiqe ....

....

Can you say the following in French? Check your answers by listening to track 37.   ◉ 37

1. Are there any nibbles?
2. A few olives, please.

....

Make sure you've understood what is being said in these two short dialogues. Focus on the following: ◉ 38

1. What hot drinks are ordered in the first exchange? ....
   ....

2. In the second exchange, is the order for white wine and olives or red wine
   and peanuts? ....

....

Fill in the gaps in this conversation between a barman and a female customer. We've given you some first letters:

Serveur	Vous d ...., madame?
Client	Un apéritif et des chips, s'il vous plaît.
Serveur	Autre .... ?
Client	Oui, deux t..................... au saumon.
Serveur	Et c..................... b.....................? Avec ou sans alcool?
Client	Oui, un v..................... de v..................... blanc.

Remember that the main points in this unit were:

1. asking if someone has something – **Il y a une carte?**
2. asking if an appetizer contains something – **Il y a de la viande?**
3. ordering food and drinks – **Je voudrais .../ Je prende .../Pour moi ...**

. . . .

Now see how good your memory is. Can you give the French names for these appetizers?

1.

....

2.

....

3.

....

4.

....

5.

....

6.

....

Choose the correct option to complete each sentence:

1. Bonsoir. Je voudrais deux .... au saumon.

   a. restaurants b. tartines c. cacahuètes d. chips

2. Il n'y .... pas de viande dans celles-ci.

   a. est b. suis c. a d. c'est

3. .... végétarienne.

   a. Je suis b. C'est c. Celui-ci est d. Je voudrais

4. Pour moi, un .... crème, s'il vous plaît.

   a. bière b. vin c. café d. apéritif

Au restaurant
In the restaurant

6

We'll be focusing on the restaurant experience in France, looking at the language you'll need to order what you want, as well as highlighting some of the regional delicacies you might fancy trying.

Traveller's tip

Sitting down to a meal in France – whether in a top-class restaurant or a humble set-menu bar – is not an experience to be rushed. Every meal is important in France: from the **croissant** or **brioche** and **café** to lunch and dinner, they are to be enjoyed by the whole family. You may find that dinner is eaten a little later than you may be used to: dinner can start as late as 7.30–8.30pm and go on until after midnight in large cities.

Many visitors' first taste of French food is the **plat du jour**, a daily main dish included in restaurant menus.

Further up market, restaurants such as Pierre Gagnaire's and Guy Savoy's, both in Paris, have been making waves internationally for the excellence and originality of their cuisine. The 1–3 star establishments in France offer traditional, but exquisite fare, and often **nouvelle cuisine**.

Each region of France is fiercely and justifiably proud of its local dishes. In the south, **la bouillabaisse** fish soup is typical, while the east specialises in **choucroute** ((hot sauerkraut) and out west, Britanny is renowned for its **crêpes**. Such regional dishes are well worth trying, as well as sampling locally produced food and drink – **les produits du terroir**. Most regions of France are famous for their cheese – **Cantal, Comté, Reblochon** or **Roquefort** or for their wines, but there is also **le foie gras, le poulet de Bresse** – tasty chicken from Bresse – cider from Normandy and thousands more delicacies for your palate to discover.

In this unit we'll be sitting down to a three-course lunch and using several useful structures along the way. We'll also learn more about the conventions of ordering food.

Qu'est-ce que ...?	What is ...?
Il y a/Il n'y a pas ...	There is, there are/There isn't, there aren't
Avez-vous ...?	Do you have ...?

 ## Listen up 1

Tom and Linda go into a restaurant for lunch. Listen to the conversation they have with the waiter, which takes you through the different stages of ordering a meal.

⊙ 39

Remember that transcripts for all of the audio tracks are available online at www. collinslanguage.com/click.

Words and phrases 1

Avez-vous ...?	Do you have.../Have you got ...?/Have you ...?
table *f*	table
par ici	this way
plat *m* du jour	dish of the day
comme entrée	for starters
comme plat (principal)	for the (main) course
poulet *m*	chicken
c'est	it's
sauce *f*	sauce
oignon *m*	onion. **oignon blanc** is a 'spring onion'.

tomate _f_	tomato
poivron _m_	pepper (vegetable)
estragon _m_	tarragon
formule _f_	set menu; some restaurants offer 'starter and main course' or 'main course and dessert' set menus. Others offer a three- to six-course menu.
salade _f_ niçoise	mixed salad containing potato, egg and tuna
pomme _f_ de terre	potato. The plural is **pommes de terre**.
salade _f_ verte	green salad
thon _m_	tuna
œuf _m_	egg. In a French restaurant you're most likely to come across **œuf dur** 'hard-boiled egg' and **œuf mollet** 'soft-boiled egg'.
ail _m_	garlic
d'accord	OK
Et pour vous?	And for you?
Entendu.	Understood.
melon _m_	melon
dessert _m_	dessert
Je voudrais ...	I'd like ...
entrecôte _f_ grillée	grilled rib steak
frites _f_	chips, French fries
quelle cuisson? _f_	How do you want it cooked? (lit. 'which cooking?')
bien cuit	well done. There are four ways of cooking steak in French: **bleu** 'very rare', **saignant** 'rare', **à point** 'medium-rare', and **bien cuit** 'well-done'.
poivre _m_	pepper (condiment).
comme boissons? _f_	What would you like to drink?
bouteille _f_	bottle
eau _f_ non gazeuse	still water (lit. non-gassy water). Sparkling water is **eau gazeuse**.

🔒 Unlocking the language 1

Qu'est-ce que ...? • 'What ...?' It literally means 'what is it that ...?'
Qu'est-ce qu'il y a? ('What is there?') is literally 'what is it that there is?

Avez-vous choisi? Literally 'Have you chosen?' **Choisi** is the past of **choisir** which means 'to choose'. **Avez-vous** can also be used to mean 'do you have?' and 'have you got?': **Avez-vous un table pour deux?** 'Do you have a table for two?'

Quelle cuisson ...? **quelle** means 'which/what'. It's the feminine form. You've come across **quelle** in **à quelle heure?** The masculine form is **quel** and is useful to say 'which day?' **quel jour?** or 'which train?' **quel train?** Don't worry – both forms sound exactly the same!

↗ Your turn 1

Find expressions in the dialogue to convey the following. You can check your answers online at www.collinslanguage.com/click.

1. Have you got a table for two?
2. for starters ...
3. for the main course ...
4. What is poulet Basquaise?
5. rib steak and fries
6. Something to drink?
7. some red wine

Pronunciation Tips

bouteille, grillée
The **ill** combination sounds like the 'ye' of 'yes'. So there's no 'l' sound really when you say **bouteille** and **grillée**.

un œuf, les œufs
You say the 'f' when you're talking about one egg (*uhn uhf*), but you don't pronounce it in the plural (*lez uh*). Notice how the **o** and the **e** are joined together.

• •

Match the expressions on the left with their 'continuations' on the right:

Qu'est-ce qu'il y	pour deux?
Pour moi, le menu	désirez comme entrée?
Qu'est-ce que vous	a comme plat du jour?
Avez-vous une table	à dix-sept euros.

60   soixante

Now, using the language you've learned in the dialogue, think about ordering a range of different starters, main courses and drinks. How would you say the following? Begin each order with *pour moi …* Check your answers by listening to track 40.

1. chicken with French fries

2. grilled rib steak

3. green salad

4. hard-boiled egg

5. a glass of rosé wine

. . . .

Listen to the three customers on track 41 and make sure you have understood what their orders are. Then decide if each of the statements below is true or false:

◎ 41

1. The order is for Niçoise salad and rib steak. ....

2. The order is for green salad and chicken. ....

3. The order is for two beers and a bottle of wine. ....

Listen up 2

The couple have finished their main courses. Their waiter asks them what they'd like next. You'll hear that the conversation covers both desserts and coffees, as well as paying at the end.

⊙ 42

Words and phrases 2

Ça a été?	'How's it going?'/'How are things?' You'll often hear this in restaurants. Here, the meaning is 'How was it?'
Désirez-vous ... ?	Do you (*plural*) want ...?
dessert *m*	dessert. Make sure you pronounce it with a hard 's', as **désert** with a 'z' sound means 'desert'.
tarte *f* tatin	an upside-down apple or pear tart
glace *f*	ice cream
à la vanille *f*	vanilla-flavoured. The pronunciation of **vanille** is *vah-neeh-uh*
à la fraise *f*	strawberry-flavoured
Je ne veux rien.	I don't want anything.
l'addition *f*	the bill
gardez la monnaie	keep the change
Bonne fin de soirée	enjoy the rest of your evening

Désirez-vous …?	This asks someone (or two people) politely if they want something: **Désirez-vous des cafés?** – 'Do you want coffee?'
Il n'y a pas	Notice that the way of making **il y a** negative is simply to put **n'** and **pas** before **y** and after **a**: **il y a** – there is; **il n'y a pas** – there isn't.
de la glace, **de la** tarte tatin et **de la** crème brûlée.	**de la** means 'some'. In French, there's always either 'some', 'the' or 'a' before item of food. The equivalents of 'some' are **de la** for feminine items, **du** for masculine items, **de l'** for all singular words starting with a vowel (a, e, i, o, u) or an 'h', and **des** for plural words.
Je **ne** veux **rien**	A stage on from the use of **ne … pas**, above, is to sandwich the verb with **ne** and **rien**, to produce 'je **ne** veux **rien** – 'I don't want anything'. It might look like an ugly double negative ('I don't want nothing') but this is correct and normal in French.
Gardez la monnaie.	This is a command form, but again has a tone of politeness about it. There's no obligation to leave a tip in French bars and restaurants (people often just leave a couple of coins) but there is no harm in leaving 5–10% if you've enjoyed your meal.

✈ Your turn 2

Find the desserts and flavours hidden in these anagrams:

1. a gelc ....
2. et rat ....
3. cûrlé meèbre ....
4. reifas ....
5. livnela ....

Can you say the following in French? Check your answers by listening to the audio track. ⊙ 43

1. I don't want anything.

2. For me, an espresso.

3. The bill, please.

· ·

Listen to these short dialogues, and identify which of the options ⊙ 44
are being asked for:

1. Does the customer ask for:
   a. a coffee and a vanilla ice cream
   b. a crème brûlée and a strawberry ice cream
   c. a chocolate ice cream and a coffee?

2. Does the customer ask for:
   a. two black coffees
   b. one espresso with a dash of cream
   c. one espresso with a dash of cream and one decaffeinated coffee?

· ·

Each line below has its words in the wrong order. Use the language you've
learned in this unit to recognise the words:

1. vous l'addition plaît s'il ....

2. la voici carte ....

3. ne veux je rien ....

4. la gardez monnaie ....

Remember that the main points in this unit have been:

1. establishing what there is (on a menu) – **Il y a de la glace au chocolat?**

2. stating preferences/orders – **je voudrais la salade niçoise/je voudrais un dessert**

3. looking at restaurant conventions – **une table pour deux; l'entrée, le plat principal, le dessert; l'addition, s'il vous plaît,** etc.

• •

Now see how good your memory is. Can you give the French names for these dishes?

1. chicken from the Basque Country ....

2. mixed salad from Nice ....

3. rib steak with fries ....

4. ice cream ....

5. vanilla ....

• •

Choose the correct option to complete each sentence:

1. Avez-vous une table .... deux?

   a. par   b. pour   c. la   d. de

2. ....-vous des desserts?

   a. Moi   b. Veux   c. Désirez   d. Comme

3. .... , s'il vous plaît.

   a. Coûte   b. Combien   c. C'est   d. L'addition

4. Gardez la ....

   a. monnaie   b. euro   c. change   d. argent

Révisions 1
Revision 1

About yourself

Can you remember how to build up the following information about yourself in French, using the verb *être*?

- I am (*name*)
- I am (*nationality*) – remember to use the masculine or feminine ending of the nationality word as appropriate
- I am from (+ *town or country*)
- I am (*job/occupation*) – remember not to use an equivalent of 'a' before the job
- I am (*characteristics*) – look up some new adjectives to describe your appearance and personality traits

Listen up 1

You'd like to save your new French friends' phone numbers in your mobile but first they're helping you learn how to spell their names. Write down their names as they spell them out for you. You can refer back to the alphabet in Unit 3 if you get stuck. ⊙ 45

1. ....
2. ....
3. ....
4. ....
5. ....
6. ....

Speak out

How would you say the following in French? Check your answers by listening to the track 46. ⊙ 46

1. Are you going to Marseille?
2. Yes, I'm going to Marseille.

3. Are you going to France?

4. No, I'm not going to France.

5. Are you going to the cinema? ('cinema' is **cinéma**)

6. No, I'm going to the restaurant.

Numbers

Revise the numbers from 0 to 99 carefully. Try to spot and memorise the patterns in clusters (e.g. the teens, twenties) and look again at the more complex structures from 70 to 99.

Now try and say out loud the following French numbers. Check your answers by listening to the audio track. ⊙ 47

1.	16	6.	56
2.	20	7.	63
3.	27	8.	78
4.	30	9.	80
5.	31	10.	94

Listen up 2

Listen to some conversation extracts and answer the questions. ⊙ 48

1. What is the room number and the floor? ....

2. What is the man's phone number? ....

3. At what address is the restaurant located? ....

4. What is the reference number? ....

5. At what number is the hotel located? ....

Parler avec les gens
Talking to people

We'll go deeper into some of the structures we've already covered, to allow you to engage more fully in conversations with people you meet. We'll also learn how to speak to people in a friendlier way.

Traveller's tip

One of the trickiest barriers to overcome when you're learning French and using it to talk to people is the two different ways of saying 'you'.

In standard modern English, there is just one form: whether you're talking to one person or ten, to a prime minister or a child, the word is simply 'you'.

In French it's different. So far in this course, we've used what is known as the formal or polite form, generally used when you don't know someone very well and you want to be respectful. This has been characterised by the word **vous** (polite 'you') and a particular verb form to go with it.

In this unit we'll turn our attention to the informal, 'friendly' form, used with someone your age or younger, with whom you feel comfortable and whom you now feel you know a bit better. This is often known as the **tu** form (= informal 'you').

With practice you'll know instinctively which form to use. It's safer to start with the polite form so as not to risk offending anyone, but French people will understand that you are not being intentionally rude if you use the wrong form. They will often put you at your ease by saying **on se tutoie** ('we call each other **tu**') or **on peut se tutoyer** ('we can call each other **tu**').

In this unit we'll be looking at formal and informal ways of addressing people. We'll also be revising some earlier structures and adapting them.

Es-tu anglais(e)?	Are you English?
Vas-tu dans le centre-ville?	Are you going to the centre?
Quel âge as-tu?	How old are you?

 ## Listen up 1

On the bus, Tom and Linda bump into Michel, a man they met the previous day. They're all on their way to do some shopping, but decide to go to a bar for a quick drink first. Listen carefully, as they'll be ordering drinks and also revealing some ages!

⊙ 49

Words and phrases 1

On peut se tutoyer?	Can we call each other (lit. we can treat each other as) **tu**? Sometimes people say **on** instead of **nous** when they mean 'we'.
Je dois ...	I have to ...
faire des courses	to do some shopping
prendre un verre	to have something to drink
Je vous invite.	It's my treat (lit. I invite you). **Inviter** is 'to invite', and is one of the usual ways for someone to say that they're buying the drinks.
une bière pression	a draft (beer)

s'il te plaît	please (*informal version*)
aujourd'hui	today
anniversaire *m*	birthday
bon anniversaire	happy birthday
Si ce n'est pas indiscret ...	If you don't mind my asking ...
Quel âge as-tu?	How old are you?
J'ai 23 ans.	I'm 23.
Je suis le plus vieux du groupe.	I'm the oldest one in the group.
Ne t'en fais pas!	Don't worry!
À la vôtre!	Cheers! There are other ways of saying 'cheers' in French: informally to one person **à la tienne**! And also (**à votre**) **santé**! (lit. to your health).

🔓 Unlocking the language 1

Veux-**tu** prendre un verre?
Quel âge as-**tu**?
Tu n'es pas vieux.
Peux-**tu** ...?

We're now starting to focus on the informal style of verbs. The examples here are from very common irregular verbs (**vouloir**, **avoir**, **être**, **pouvoir**). We'll do plenty more practice, so don't worry if it's a bit confusing at first.

Peux-tu me donner ...?

Here's the informal way of asking for something. You can now compare it with the formal **Pouvez-vous me donner ...? Peux** is the **tu** form of **pouvoir**.

l'anniversaire de Linda

There's no apostrophe in French to allow us to say something like 'Linda's birthday'. Instead, we have to say 'the birthday of Linda'.

Quel âge as-tu?
J'ai 23 ans.

To ask and tell our age in French, we don't talk about 'being 23', but rather 'having 23 years'. So we use the verb **avoir** – **Quel âge as-tu**? ('What age do you have?'); **J'ai 23 ans**. ('I have 23 years').

Quel âge as-tu?
Tu as quel âge?

There are different ways to ask questions in French. There can be an inversion **Quel âge as-tu?** or no inversion **Tu as quel âge?** When inversion is used, **quel âge** comes first.

Choose the one you find the easiest! The 'inversion' way sounds more formal, though.

Find expressions in the dialogue to convey the following:

1. Can we call each other *tu*?

2. Are you going to the town centre? (*informal*)

3. What do you want? (*to two people*)

4. It's my treat.

5. Happy birthday!

6. Don't worry! (*informally*)

Pronunciation Tips

pression

This is a simple point, but often overlooked. Try to pronounce every **ss** in French as if it were ss, like the end of the word 'hiss' (rather than 'pressure' – can you feel the difference?).

tu

u is not pronounced as in English. It is more like 'ew' in 'news'. To say it, put your lips as if you were about to say 'oo', keep your lips in this position but instead say 'ee', and that will sound like a French **'u'**!

• •

Speaking informally and using *pouvoir*, how would you ask for the following? ◉ 50

Can I have ...

1. three beers, please?

2. two glasses of red wine, please?

3. a portion of olives, please?

• •

Listen to the people talking, and answer the following questions: ◉ 51

1. How old is the first speaker? ....

2. Does the second speaker use the formal or informal form of 'you'?
....

3. How old is the third speaker? ....

Formal or informal? Complete the right hand column below, supplying the informal bits of each verb. We've given you one to start off:

Formal	Informal
1. Quel âge avez-vous?	Quel âge as-tu?
2. Pouvez-vous me donner une bière?	....
3. Voulez-vous prendre un verre?	....
4. Êtes-vous nerveux?	....

Listen up 2

Florian gets chatting to Hannah, a Canadian student, in the park. Listen out for details about their jobs and studies.   ⊙ 52

Words and phrases 2

Excuse-moi	Excuse me – informal command from **excuser** (to pardon, to excuse).
perdu/perdue	lost *m/f*
pas du tout	not at all
tu es	you are (from **être**)
canadien/canadienne	Canadian *m/f*
être en vacances	to be on holiday. To go on holiday is **partir en vacances**.
j'étudie	I study (from **étudier**)
école *f* de langues *f*	language school
tu parles	you speak (from **parler**)
pratiquer	to practise
Je m'appelle Florian.	My name's Florian (lit. I call myself Florian).

guide	Person working as a guide (**un guide** for a man, **une guide** for a woman); pronounced 'geed'.
tu as	You have (*informal*)
j'ai	I have
emploi *m*	job/employment
travailler	to work
peu de temps *m* libre	very little free time
On commande?	Shall we order? (food or drinks)
jus *m* d'orange *f*	orange juice (lit. juice of orange)

 ## Unlocking the language 2

as
Tu as deux emplois?

This is the informal 'you' form of **avoir**. Let's summarise this verb:
j'ai – I have
tu as – you have (*informal*)
vous avez – you have (*polite or plural*)
il/elle a – he/she/it has

es
Tu es perdue?
Tu es en vacances?
Tu es étudiante.
Tu n'es pas d'ici.
Je suis canadienne.
Je suis professeur.

This is the informal 'you' form of **être**. Here's a summary of this verb:
je suis – I am
tu es – you are (*informal*)
vous êtes – you are (*polite or plural*)
il/elle a – he/she/it is

j'aime travailler

The **j'aime** structure works not only with things (**j'aime le vin blanc/l'art**) but also with activities expressed as verbs: **j'aime travailler** ('I like working' – lit. 'I like to work.')

Let's recap how to use verbs. To speak using **je** ('I'), **il** and **elle** ('he', 'she', 'it') with regular verbs ending with -**er**, like **aimer** ('to like'), or **parler** ('to speak'), just remove the **r**:

j'aime ('I like') and **il aime** ('he likes')
je parle ('I speak') and **elle parle** ('she speaks')

To use a regular -**er** verb with **tu** ('you'), remove the **r** and add an **s**:
tu aimes ('you like') and **tu parles** ('you speak')

Voilà!

Here are some anagrams of informal French verbs (ending in -s or -x) for you to unravel:

1. lepsar ....
2. uxev ....
3. sa ....
4. se ....
5. exup ....

••

Can you say the following (informally) in French? Check your answers ⊙ 53 by listening to track 53.

1. Are you on holiday?
2. I'm on holiday.
3. Not at all.
4. Don't worry.

••

Listen to the four descriptions (A, B, C and D) and match what is ⊙ 54 said in each case with the corresponding photo. Write their names if you can catch them:

1.

....

2.

....

3.

....

4.

....

Below are some formal (polite) questions. Use the language you've learned above to change each verb to the informal style:

1. Voulez-vous prendre un verre? ....

2. Avez-vous beaucoup de temps libre? ....

3. Aimez-vous la cuisine italienne? ....

4. Parlez-vous anglais? ....

Let's recap

In this unit we've looked at the difference between polite and informal ways of addressing people. We've also studied the way to ask and state how old someone is. Here are some model sentences to help you remember:

Êtes-vous canadienne? (*polite*)

Es-tu canadienne? (*informal*)

Voulez-vous aller au cinéma? (*polite*)

Veux-tu aller au cinéma? (*informal*)

Quel âge avez-vous? (*polite*)

Tu as quel âge? (*informal*)

J'ai trente-quatre ans. ('*I*' – *first person singular*)

Now see how good your memory is for numbers. Each of the numbers below is misspelt. Try and spot the error, then practise saying the corrected version.

1. 33   trente-trios ....

2. 44   quarente-quatre ....

3. 55   cinquante-cink ....

4. 66   sioxante-six ....

Choose the correct option to complete each sentence:

1. Tu .... nerveux aujourd'hui.

   a. es   b. as   c. est   d. ai

2. Tu .... 23 ans.

   a. es   b. as   c. est   d. ai

3. Tu .... prendre un verre?

   a. as   b. avez   c. voulez   d. veux

4. Tu .... aller au cinéma?

   a. pouvez   b. peux   c. as   d. avez

Faire des courses
Out shopping

8

We'll cover the language you'll need when you go out shopping, and take a look at what sorts of shops you can expect to find.

Traveller's tip

At some point in your trip to France, you're bound to fancy a saunter around the shops to see what's on offer and perhaps pick up a bargain.

The first thing you'll notice in French cities is that whilst large chains are of course present, there are some independent boutiques. Whereas the UK, for example, is infamous for having branches of the same shops on every high street, France's shopping streets offer plenty of traditional food shops and small businesses.

The one department store no city centre is without is **Monoprix** – where you can get pretty much anything – and you'll often find the multimedia and bookstore **FNAC**.

Paris is one of the world's major centres for the fashion industry, and there's something to suit every budget: from the *haute couture* boutiques like **Chanel**, **Dior**, **Yves Saint-Laurent**, **Jean-Paul Gaultier**, **Agnès B.**, to the **grands magasins** – department stores – such as **les Galeries Lafayettes**, **le Printemps**, and **le Bon Marché**.

For *prêt-à-porter* items you might want to have a look at some French designers and labels: **Comptoirs des Cotonniers**, **Kookaï**, **Esprit**, or **Caroll**, and so many more.

Shopping isn't just about clothes, of course, and the major brands of perfume, leather goods (**maroquinerie**), shoes and household goods have boutiques in most French towns.

Store opening hours are generally quite long, with most staying open until 7pm, or later in tourist areas. Be aware that some smaller shops close for lunch, usually between about 12.00 and 2.30pm, which reflects the importance of the eating experience we saw in Unit 6.

Whether you're a shopaholic or a retail novice, a dip into the chic boutiques of French shopping is always a delightful experience.

In this unit we'll be revising some of the structures we met in earlier units, and will look carefully at the language you'll need to browse and make purchases.

Avez-vous ...?   Have you got ...?
Je voudrais/Je préfère I want/I prefer

Listen up 1

Stephanie is looking to buy a shirt for herself. Listen to the dialogues on track 55 to see how she gets on. Try and pick out the price of the item she buys.

⊙ 55

Words and phrases 1

Qu'est-ce que vous cherchez?	What are you looking for? **chercher** is 'to look for' – you don't need an extra word for 'for'.
chemise *f*	shirt
blanc/blanche	white *m/f*
(en) coton *m*	(made of) cotton
medium	medium *m/f*
taille *f*	size (of clothing)
Je peux l'essayer?	Can I try it on?
bien sûr	of course
trop petit	too small
Je ne la prends pas.	I'll leave it.
Elle coûte combien?	How much is it?

trente-neuf euros	39 euros. The symbol always follows the price: **39 €** Euros are separated from **cents** with a comma: **56, 45 €**
C'est un peu cher.	It's a bit expensive.
un/une autre	other/another *m/f*
joli/jolie	pretty *m/f*
Je la prends.	I'll take it.
Suivez-moi jusqu'à la caisse, s'il vous plaît.	Come to the till, please.

🔓 Unlocking the language 1

adjectives

You'll notice that in *Words and Phrases* above, we've given you **blanc** and **blanche** for 'white'. Which one you use depends on whether the item being described is masculine or feminine. **Chemise** is feminine, so we say **une chemise blanche**. 'A white sweater' *(masculine)* would be **un pull blanc**. You'll get used to it with practice.

this (one)

There's also a masculine/feminine thing going on here. 'This shirt' *(feminine)* is **cette chemise**, but 'this sweater' *(masculine)* would be **ce pull**. If you don't want to repeat the word **chemise** and prefer to say 'this one', you can use **celle-ci**. You can find this last variant in the third line of the dialogue.

it

In this dialogue, 'it' refers to **la chemise**, a feminine word. This why the customer says **je *la* prends** and **je ne *la* prends pas**.

If 'it' was referring to **un pull**, the customer would say **je *le* prends** or **je ne *le* prends pas**.

In the case of, **je peux *l'*essayer**, the **l'** could refer to both **la chemise** and **le pull**.

Find expressions in the dialogue to convey the following. The ◉ 55
answers to all of the activities are available online at
www.collinslanguage.com/click.

1. What are you looking for?

2. Here's one.

3. Can I try it on?

4. I'll leave it, thanks.

5. Is it cotton?

6. I'll take it.

Pronunciation Tips

taille

taille is another example of the **-ill** sound, when
the double 'l' is not pronounced. It sounds like the
'ye' of 'yes'.

peu, euros, peux, neuf

eu sounds like 'euh', like the **œu** combination you
heard in Unit 6.

cher

For this one you do pronounce the 'r' at the end, so
that it sounds a bit like 'share'. The feminine form,
chère, sounds exactly the same.

• •

It's time to revise our numbers so that we can state and understand ◉ 56
prices. How would you say the following prices? Begin each sentence
with *Ça coûte* – this costs – and end it with *euros*. Check your answers
by listening to the audio track.

1. 19 ....

2. 24 ....

3. 35 ....

4. 47 ....

5. 58 ....

• •

Listen to the people talking and make sure you have understood ◉ 57
what each person is saying. Then answer the following questions:

1. What's the problem in the first example? ....

2. Does the second shopper buy the item? ....

3. What does the shop assistant ask the shopper to do in the third example?

....

Listen up 2

It's time for more shopping, and there are some more decisions to be made. Listen to the conversations; in the first dialogue the shop assistant is using the polite form of address, while in the second dialogue, the customer and the shop assistant know each other and are comfortable using the 'tu' form.

⊙ 58

Words and phrases 2

plateau *m*	tray, platter
lequel	which one?
vous préférez/je préfère	you prefer/I prefer
Je vous l'emballe?	'Shall I wrap it for you?' You may sometimes be asked **C'est pour offrir?** (Is it a gift for someone?) so that the shop assistant can gift-wrap it beautifully for you at no extra cost.
c'est gentil	(that's) very kind (of you)
ces	these *m/f*
chaussures *f*	shoes
Tu paies comment? Comment paies-tu?	How are you paying?
en espèces	in cash (you may also hear **en cash**).
tape ton code	Tap in your PIN code (secret number). The formal variants would be **composez** or **entrez votre ...** It's also common to hear tape (z) ton/votre code PIN.
ça y est	that's it – done
belle	gorgeous
non?	aren't they? French people often add a simple **non?** to the end of statements to turn them into questions, just like we do in English with the tags 'isn't it?', 'can't she?', 'shouldn't I?', etc. The French system is much simpler!
à bientôt	See you (again) soon

préfère/préférez   We've got used to seeing pairs of verb forms, where the one ending in **-e** is for 'I' and the other one ending in **-z** is for 'you': e.g. **je cherche** ('I am looking for') and **vous cherchez** ('you are looking for'). Here's another pair, belonging to the verb **préférer** ('to prefer').

Notice the change in accents and in pronunciation between the form for **je préfère** (*pray-ferre*) and the form for **vous préférez** (*pray-fay-ray*).

Plural adjectives   You'll have noticed that we've said **ces chaussures** for 'these shoes'. Just as 'this' becomes 'these' in English, French has a means of denoting plurals: **ce** ('this') and the feminine form **cette** both become **ces** ('these').

Once again the final **s** in **ces** is silent, except before a word beginning with a vowel (a, e, i, o, u) or an 'h'. So you'd say **ces hotels**: *say zoh-tel*.

Notice also that whereas the **chemise** in the first dialogue was **belle**, the **chaussures** here are **belles**. It all matches up!

Your turn 2

Think about the use of *blanc, blanche, blancs, blanches* **to describe various things as being white. Which would be the correct form in each of the cases below?**

1. un plateau . . . .
2. une chemise . . . .
3. des plateaux . . . .
4. des chemises . . . .

. . . .

Can you say the following in French? We're using the polite form. 59
Check your answers by listening to the audio track.

1. Which one do you prefer?   3. In cash.
2. Shall I wrap it up for you?

Make sure you've understood what is being said in these short dialogues. Listen out specifically for the following information:

◉ 60

1. How much is the item in the first exchange? ....
2. How will the second shopper be paying? ....

Remember that the main points in this unit have been:

1. stating what you're looking for in a shop – **je cherche une chemise blanche**
2. wanting and preferring – **je voudrais cette chemise – je préfère ce pull**
3. work on this/these – **ce pull/cette chemise/ces chaussures/ces chemises**
4. work on 'it' – **je peux l'essayer/je la prends /je ne la prends pas**

· ·

Now see how good your memory is. Thinking about *une chemise*, how would you say the following?

1. I want a shirt.
2. I want a white shirt.
3. I prefer this shirt.
4. It's pretty.

· ·

Choose the correct option to complete each sentence:

1. .... chemises sont belles.

    a. Ce   b. Cette   c. Ces

2. Je préfère .... plateaux.

    a. ce   b. cette   c. ces

3. .... pull est beau.

    a. Ce   b. Cette   c. Ces

4. Je voudrais .... chemise.

    a. ce   b. cette   c. ces

Un peu de culture
A bit of culture

9

We'll take a trip to a French museum, looking at what's on offer, what you can expect to pay, and how to say what you need to say there.

Traveller's tip

Once you've had your initial burst of *apéritifs*, *amuse-bouches* and shopping, it's time to check out the wealth of historical and contemporary cultural options on offer. Your hotel or the tourist information office (**syndicat d'initiative** or **office du tourisme**) will have leaflets telling you where to head for.

In fact, French cities have so much history visible in their streets and buildings that it's not always necessary to visit a museum to get your culture fix. You can plan your day to take in strolls around particular **quartiers** (districts or quarters), where you can not only savour the flavour of an area, but also stop off for a **plat du jour**.

The larger cities, especially Paris, Lyon, Marseille and Toulouse, have a huge range of art galleries (**galeries**) and museums (**musées**) to cover all tastes. Look out for one of various types of city card, giving you discounted entry into certain museums.

One of the great opportunities to discover historical buildings which are normally closed to the public is in September, during the European Heritage Days.

As is the case with shopping, you'll find museum opening times are often generous, allowing you to absorb the contents without feeling rushed. If you fancy staying on to have something to eat in the museum's restaurant – perhaps on a terrace overlooking the city – then so much the better.

In this unit we'll learn three new structures: saying that we like something, that we're going to do something, and that we want to do something.

J'aime ...	I like ...
Je vais visiter ...	I'm going to visit ...
Je veux/voudrais aller à ...	I want to go to ...

Listen up 1

Tom is at the reception desk in his hotel asking for information about a museum. We learn about the museum's location, its opening hours and admission price. See if you can pick these out as you listen.

◉ 61

Transcripts for the audio tracks on the CD are available online at www.collinslanguage.com/click.

Words and phrases 1

Je veux aller/Voulez-vous aller?	I want to go/Do you want to go?
musée *m*	museum
art *m* moderne	modern art
bien sûr que c'est possible	of course it's possible
Je vais vous écrire les directions.	I'm going to jot down the directions for you.
C'est très gentil.	That's very kind (of you).
aujourd'hui	today
Aimez-vous ...?	Do you like ...?
j'aime beaucoup	I like it (a lot)
moi aussi	so do I/me too
entrée *f*	admission; entry
réduction *f*	discount/concession
Quelles sont les heures d'ouverture?	What are the opening hours?
il est ouvert	it is open

de neuf heures du matin	from 9am
à cinq heures de l'après-midi	until 5pm
voir	to see
tout	all, everything
faire une promenade	to go for a stroll

Unlocking the language 1

je veux aller	'I want to go'. Up to now, we've seen **je veux/je voudrais** used with an item – **je veux une glace** ('I want an ice cream'). You can also use it with another verb to state what you want to do – **je veux aller…** ('I want to go…').
je vais aller	Similarly, you can talk about what you're going to do by using a part of **aller** (e.g. **je vais** 'I'm going') + another verb, e.g. **je vais prendre un café** (I'm going to have a coffee), **je vais aller…** (I'm going to go …).
Aimez-vous …? J'aime …	**Aimer** can be used like **préférer** and **chercher**. You just have to put what you like after it, e.g. **j'aime l'art moderne**. You can add **beaucoup**, e.g. **j'aime beaucoup…** 'I like …very much'. To say that you don't like something, just use **ne** and **pas**: **je n' aime pas le vin rosé**.

Your turn 1

Find expressions in the dialogue to convey the following. The answers to all of the activities are available online at www.collinslanguage.com/click.

⊙ 61

1. I want to go to the museum.
2. I'm going to jot down the directions.
3. That's very kind of you.
4. Do you like modern art?
5. Yes, I like it a lot.
6. There's a discount.
7. Now I'm going to go for a stroll.

Pronunciation Tips

écrire, réduction, entrée après-midi

As you saw earlier, accents on **e** in French change the pronunciation slightly:

é sounds like 'ay' in 'say'.

è sounds like the 'e' in 'egg'.

neuf heures

Like in English, words can run together in French, which explains why you can get the impression of hearing one word when in fact there are two. In this case, the French say 'nuh-vuhr'. The **f** is pronounced like a v.

Let's have a look at the new structures we've learned in
Unlocking the Language 1. How would you say the following?
There are some hints provided in brackets. Check your
answers by listening to the audio track. ⊙ 62

1. I want to go to the art gallery. (à la galerie d'art)

2. I'm going to have a glass of wine. (boire un verre de vin)

3. I like art. (l'art)

. . . .

Listen to the people talking, and make sure you have understood
what they're saying. Pay particular attention to the following: ⊙ 63

1. What does the first person like and dislike? ....

2. Which building is the second person going to see? ....

3. What does the third person want to eat? ....

. . . .

Quelles sont les heures d'ouverture? Match the opening times in the left-
hand column with the corresponding figures on the right:

Le musée du Louvre est ouvert de neuf heures du matin à six heures du soir.	10.30am–12.30pm + 2.00–6.30pm
Le château de Chambord est ouvert de neuf heures du matin à sept heures et demie du soir.	11.00am–8.00pm
Le petit musée de Guignol est ouvert de dix heures et demie du matin à midi et demie, et de deux heures de l'après-midi à six heures et demie du soir.	9.00am–6.00pm
Le musée du Pont du Gard est ouvert de onze heures du matin à huit heures du soir.	9.00am–7.30pm

Le château de Chambord

Listen up 2

During his visit to a museum, Tom buys his entry ticket, gets some
assistance from a guide and later strikes up a conversation with
another visitor. Listen to the dialogues.

⊙ 64

Words and phrases 2

adulte	adult *m/f*
alors	so/therefore
vingt pour cent	20%
contemporain	contemporary
section *f*	section
grand/grande	big
dans la salle *f* principale	in the main hall
dépliant *m*	leaflet
sculpture *f*	sculpture
expert/experte	expert *m/f*
exposition *f*	exhibition
commentaire *m*	commentary – it can also mean simply 'comment'.
reste *m*	rest (remainder)
nous nous retrouvons	**se retrouver** here means 'to meet again'. So here we are saying 'Shall we meet at 3.00?'
à trois heures	See you at 3.00 (lit. at 3.00)

Unlocking the language 2

nous **y** allons

Y means 'there'. In French, you always have to say where
you are going to; this is why **y** ('there') is used here. It
literally means 'we are going **there**'.

nous allons
nous retrouvons

These are verb forms indicating that 'we' are doing the
action. Let's take a moment to summarise the various
'persons' of some of the main verbs we've met:

	I	**you**	**we**
être	suis	êtes	sommes
avoir	ai	avez	avons
aller	vais	allez	allons
vouloir	veux	voulez	voulons
préférer	préfère	préférez	préférons

Use the words in the box to fill the gaps in the sentences below. It's an informal dialogue:

c'est   *aujourd'hui*   *il y a*

tu veux   *nous nous retrouvons*   *aimes*

.... une exposition d'art contemporain .... au musée.

.... très intéressant. Tu .... l'art contemporain?

Si .... y aller, ... à onze heures.

• •

Can you say the following in French? Check your answers by listening to the audio track.   ⦿ 65

1. I prefer sculpture.

2. I'm not an expert.

3. Shall we meet here at two o'clock?

• •

Make sure you've understood what is being said in these short dialogues on track 66.   ⦿ 66

1. How much is it to get in? ....

2. What discount is offered with the card? ....

3. In the second exchange, until what time is the building open? ....

Each line below has its words in the wrong order. Use the language you've learned in this unit to work out what's wrong:

1. au aller contemporain veux d' musée je art ....

2. sculpture ne mais pas suis aime je expert j' la ....

3. une nous à deux allons exposition à heures ....

Let's recap

In this unit we've looked at what we want to do, what we are going to do, and what we like. Here are some model sentences to help you remember:

J'aime l'art moderne./Je n'aime pas l'art moderne.

Je (ne) veux (pas) aller au musée.

Je vais visiter une galerie.

....

Choose the correct option to complete each sentence:

1. Vous avez .... pour cent de réduction.

   a. grand   b. dix   c. cette   d. non

2. Le musée n' .... pas ouvert aujourd'hui.

   a. suis   b. sont   c. est   d. êtes

3. L'entrée .... combien?

   a. coûte   b. euros   c. est   d. sont

4. Je veux tout ....

   a. être   b. voir   c. musée   d. aller

Dégustation de vin
Wine tasting

10

We'll look at the language you'll need to ask for information about visiting a wine cellar, as well as learning something about one of the country's most famous drinks!

In this unit we'll be revising some of the structures we've learned in earlier units, including directions, prices and times. We'll also look at words and phrases associated with wine tasting, including some useful expressions for giving your opinion.

Pour aller au domaine?	How do I get to the wine estate?
Il faut ...	You have to ...
À quelle heure est la visite?	What time is the visit?
Je le trouve très fort.	I find it very strong.

 ## Listen up 1

Tom is a bit of a wine buff, so he wants to visit a few wine cellars and do some wine tasting during his holiday in France. Listen to the dialogues. First, he asks a local for directions to a wine cellar. ⊙ 67

Tom and Linda then buy some tickets for the wine cellar and wine museum. ⊙ 68

In the wine grower's courtyard, Tom asks an employee for directions. They are both young, so they speak to each other informally using *tu*. ⊙ 69

Words and phrases 1

domaine *m*	estate, domain
il faut	you have to
continuer	to continue, to keep on
ensuite le domaine est tout près	then the estate is very near
vigne *f*	vine, vineyard
environ	about/approximately (time and distances)
visite *f*	visit

billet *m* d'entrée	ticket (for entry to a museum – see also Unit 9).
tenez	here you are (lit. 'hold')
rester	to stay
dégustation *f*	tasting
alors	then

 ## Unlocking the language 1

Pour aller a …	'How do I get to …?' (lit. 'to go to …?') This phrase is very useful for asking directions.
Il faut …	'You have to …' This is a new verb: **falloir**. It is only used with **il**. It literally means 'it's mandatory to' or 'it is necessary to', but it simply means 'you should', 'you have to' or 'you need'.
Elle/C'est à cinq heures et demie.	'It's at 5.30.' To say that something 'is' (in the sense of 'takes place' or 'happens') at a particular time, we use the verb **être** followed by **à** ('at').
tenez	This is the formal or plural command form of **tenir** (to hold), but it's courteous and normal, nonetheless. It can mean 'here you are', e.g. when someone is giving you tickets or change. The informal way is **tiens**.

 ## Your turn 1

Find expressions in the dialogues to convey the following. ⊙ 67–69
The answers to the activities in this booklet are available online at www.collinslanguage.com/click.

1. To get to the Couron wine estate, please?
2. What time is the visit?
3. How much is it?
4. That's 4 euros.
5. It's on the left, 20 metres away.
6. Would you like to stay? *(informal)*

Pronunciation Tip

pour aller
à quelle heure
quatre euros

Like in English, many French words are run together when spoken, which makes the language difficult to understand at times. Notice that you hear *pooralay* for **pour aller**, *ah keluhr* for **à quelle heure** or *katruhroh* for **quatre euros**. Don't worry: the more you listen to French people speaking, you'll get to understand what they're saying more easily – and may even start running words together like the locals!

Listen to these snippets of conversation and make sure you have understood what is said by answering these questions: 70

1. When is the visit in the first example?

2. In the second example, how many tickets are bought?

3. What directions are given to get to the wine estate in the third example?

. . . .

Match the French directions on the left with the English directions on the right. The map may help you:

a. C'est au bout de la rue.   It's there, on the right.

b. C'est à gauche, à soixante mètres.   It's very near here.

c. C'est tout près d'ici.   It's at the end of the street.

d. C'est là, à droite.   It's on the left, 60 metres away.

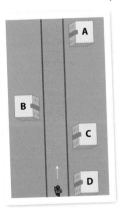

Listen up 2

Inside the wine cellar just after the visit, Tom and Linda chat with the wine producer. His name is Pascal and he's a bit older than they are, so they use the polite form. Listen to the dialogue.

⊙ 71

Words and phrases 2

Qu'est-ce que vous pensez de ...?	What do you think of ...?
cave *f*	wine cellar. Many French homes also have a **cave**, a small storage room for keeping wine or other personal possessions.
impressionnant/impressionnante	impressive *m/f*
bon/bonne	good *m/f*
je pense que	I think that
meilleur/meilleure	better *m/f*
goûter	to taste
Qu'est-ce que vous en pensez?	What do you think about it/them?
fruité/fruitée	fruity
assez	quite
léger/légère	light *m/f*
C'est vrai.	It's true.
cépage *m*	grape variety, type of vine
différent/différente	different
je le trouve ...	I find it ...
fort/forte	strong *m/f*
le premier	the first one. The feminine form is **la première**.

moi aussi	me too
plus	more
encore	again
délicieux/délicieuse	delicious *m/f*
aussi	too
moi non plus	me neither
J'ai un peu trop bu.	I have drunk a bit too much.
acheter	to buy
bouteille *f*	bottle

 ## Unlocking the language 2

Qu'est-ce que vous pensez de ...? Qu'est-ce que vous en pensez?	'What do you think of ...?' A great way of asking someone their opinion on what follows – in this case **cette cave** ('the wine cellar').
	Otherwise you could say **Qu'est-ce que vous en pensez?** which means 'What do you think?' Informally, it becomes **Qu'est-ce que tu en penses?**
meilleur/meilleure	In English, 'good' becomes 'better' when making a comparison. In French, **bon(ne)** becomes **meilleur(e)**.
plus	**Plus** means 'more'; here, **moins** means 'less' and **aussi** means 'as, equally', e.g. **ce vin est aussi bon** 'this wine is equally good'.
je pense que	'I think that ...' In English, 'that' can be omitted, e.g. 'I think it's true', but its French equivalent '**que**' is never omitted: **je pense que c'est vrai**.
je le trouve	Like for **la** and **le** in Unit 8, **le** means 'it'. To speak about **la chemise**, you say **je la trouve**.
	Trouve is the **je** form of the verb **trouver** 'to find'. The useful question linked to this reply is **Vous le/la trouvez comment?** another way of asking 'What do you think about it?'
moi aussi moi non plus	**Moi aussi** is 'me too' and **moi non plus** 'me neither'. You'll often hear the French use **moi** to emphasise the way they're feeling or what they think of something, e.g. **J'ai faim, moi!** ('I'm really hungry!), **Moi, j'adore cette couleur!** ('I absolutely adore that colour!')

Le dîner **était** délicieux.	**était** is the past form of **être** for **il/elle**. It's very useful to speak about how something was in the past.
le premier	**premier** is 'first'. The following numbers are quite easy to memorise: just add **-ième** at the end of the numbers, i.e. **deux** 'two' becomes **deuxième** 'second', **trois** 'three' becomes **troisième**, and so on.

 ## Your turn 2

Here are some anagrams of French words associated with wine tasting for you to unravel.

1. tiréfu ....
2. tofr ....
3. greél ....
4. élicuxedi ....
5. tibelolue ....

· ·

Can you say the following in French? Check your answers by listening to the audio track. ⊙ 72

1. I prefer the first one. ....
2. The dinner was delicious. ....
3. I have had a bit too much to drink. ....
4. What do you think? ....

· ·

Make sure you've understood what is being said in the expressions you'll hear: ⊙ 73

1. What is the wine like? ....
2. Which wine does the person prefer and why? ....
3. How many bottles would the person like? Of which colour? ....
4. What is the fourth speaker asking you? ....

Each line below has its words in the wrong order. Use the language you've learned in this unit to work out what's wrong:

1. pense fort trop je qu' est il ....

2. trop un j'ai peu bu ....

3. le je troisième préfère ....

 Let's recap

In this unit we've looked at what we *have to do*, and how to give your opinion. Here are some model sentences to help you remember:

Il faut continuer jusqu'au bout de la rue.

Je pense qu'il est très bon.

Je le trouve meilleur.

· ·

Now see how good your memory is. Each of the sentences below has one error. Try and spot it, then practise saying the corrected version.

1. Je voudrais aller domaine.

2. La visite est cinq heures.

3. Le vin est très bonne.

4. Deux entrée, s'il vous plaît.

5. Pour le visite du musée?

Use one of the following words to fill each of the gaps below:

rester   *quelle*   *heures*   *vins*   *goûter*

rosé   *cave*   *visite*   *billet*   *délicieux*

- Votre .... est impressionnante et vos .... sont

  .... Je voudrais .... pour la ....

  du musée. Elle est à .... heure?

- A trois .... Voulez-vous un .... d'entrée?

- Oui. Mais je voudrais .... votre .... maintenant.

- D'accord.

. . . .

Choose the correct option to complete each sentence:

1. Qu'est-ce que vous pensez .... ce vin?

   a. à   **b.** de   **c.** sur   **d.** que

2. Qu'est-ce que vous .... goûter?

   a. préfère   **b.** préfères   **c.** préférez   **d.** préférer

3. Je préfère le premier. Et toi? ....

   a. Moi aussi   **b.** Moi non plus   **c.** Et moi   **d.** Moi encore

4. Nous voulons .... dix bouteilles.

   a. rester   **b.** continuer   **c.** goûter   **d.** acheter

La vie nocturne
Nightlife

11

We'll consider some options for extending your days in France into the night. Having had an aperitif in Unit 5 and a meal in Unit 6, we'll now be paying a visit to a lounge bar for a nightcap and a bit of live jazz.

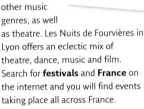

In this unit we'll be learning the language of making suggestions, and also looking at ways of saying what events are happening.

On pourrait sortir prendre un verre. We could go out for a drink.

Allons dans la rue principale. Let's go to the main street.

Il y a un groupe qui joue ce soir. There's a band playing tonight.

Listen up 1

Tom and Linda are with their new friend Michel, and they're wondering what to do after dinner. See if you can pick out where they head for. ◉ 74

A little later on, they're lucky enough to find a bar with live music. ◉ 75

Transcripts for the audio tracks on the CD are available online at www.collinslanguage.com/click.

Words and phrases 1

je ne sais pas	I don't know
On pourrait sortir prendre un verre.	We could go out for a drink.
Tu connais un endroit sympa?	Do you know a nice place? **sympa** is short for **sympathique**, which means 'pleasant' or 'friendly' rather than 'sympathetic'.
Allons dans la rue principale.	Let's go to the main street.
là-bas	over there
pas mal de bars	(it's) not bad for bars
On y va?	Shall we go?
On y va.	Let's go.
allez	come on
ce soir *m*	tonight

un groupe joue	a group is playing
On va dans ce café?	Shall we go into this café?
C'est quel style de musique?	What style of music is it?
jazz *m*	jazz
allons-y	let's go
table *f*	table
bar *m*	bar/counter
gin tonic *m*	gin and tonic
avec beaucoup de glaçons *m*	with a lot of ice
On peut lui prendre ...	We can order ... for him.
bonne idée	good idea

Unlocking the language 1

on pourrait/ on peut ...	'We could/can ...' These are standard ways in French of making suggestions as to what we can do. **peut** and **pourrait** come from the verb **pouvoir** ('to be able', incorporating ideas of 'can', 'could', etc.) They are used for 'can' in terms of permission (**on peut entrer** – 'we're allowed to go in') and in many contexts of possibility/ability (**on pourrait aller au musée** – 'we can/could go to the museum').
Tu connais un endroit sympa?	'Do you know a nice place?' **connaître** is used for 'to know' when we mean being acquainted with a person or a place.
Allons ...	'Let's go ...' **Allons** is the inviting and positive command for of **aller**. This polite suggestion is formed with the present tense of the verbs without the word **nous**.
Je ne sais pas.	'I don't know.' **Savoir** is used for 'to know' when we mean knowing a fact and how to do things.
On **y** va. Allons-**y**!	'Let's go!' Sometimes **y** refers to a specific place, i.e. 'there' or 'inside'. But often **On y va?** simply means 'Shall we get going?'

In French, there are two ways to say 'we', **nous** and **on**. This is quite flexible. Feel free to use the one you prefer. Generally though **on** sounds more informal.

Pronunciation Tip

table 'prendre' être

French words ending with –**ble**, –**dre** or –**tre** are lightly pronounced; it's as if you whispered these final sounds. So if you say the part of the words just before –**ble**, –**dre** or –**tre** louder, you'll sound like a French person!

 Your turn 1

Find expressions in the dialogues to convey the following. The answers to the activities are available online at www.collinslanguage.com/click.   ◉ 74–75

1. What do you want to do now?

2. We could go out for a drink.

3. Do you know a nice place?

4. A band's playing tonight.

5. Shall we go into this bar?

6. Let's go.

• •

Match the names of the drinks with the photos:

1. un verre de champagne

2. un gin tonic

3. une pression

a.

b.

c.

How would you say the following? Check your answers by listening to the audio track. 76

1. What do you want to drink? *(use the informal form)*

2. Let's go.

3. with a lot of ice

· ·

Listen to the people talking, and make sure you have understood what they're saying. Here are some questions to guide you: 77

1. What does the first person want with her gin and tonic? ....

2. What drink does the second person order? ....

3. What is happening tonight, and at what time? ....

· ·

Match the suggestions on the left with the activities on the right.

1. On pourrait sortir prendre ...	commander des bières?
2. On peut ...	ce bar.
3. Tu veux ...	un verre.
4. Allons dans ...	aller au cinéma, Ariane?

 ## Listen up 2

Later the same evening Tom, Linda and Michel are having fun in the jazz bar. Listen out for more drinks, the possibility of a dance, and arrangements for getting back to the hotel. 78

Words and phrases 2

chanteur/chanteuse	singer *m/f*
elle chante	she sings – from **chanter**, 'to sing'.
vraiment	really
mignon/mignonne	good-looking, cute
On pourrait commander d'autres boissons?	We could order some more drinks? **Commander** means 'to order'.
Vous voulez boire autre chose?	Do you fancy something else to drink?
danser	to dance
ce n'est pas grave	it doesn't matter
allez	come on
toilettes *f*	Toilet – you may see or hear **toilettes** or **WC** used to indicate the restrooms in public buildings. The gents' toilet is **Hommes**, the ladies' is **Dames**.
j'ai chaud/j'ai sommeil	I'm hot/I'm sleepy
je suis fatigué/fatiguée	I'm tired *m/f* – this is used more for bodily weariness; **j'ai sommeil** (see above) refers to feeling sleepy.
On appelle un taxi?	Shall we call a taxi?
rentrer	to return/go back/go home

 Unlocking the language 2

Tu aimes	'You like' – **aimes** is the **tu** form of **aimer**.
J'ai chaud/ sommeil	'I'm hot/sleepy.'

A number of expressions that would start with 'I am' in English begin with **j'ai** ('I have') in French. Here, 'we're actually saying 'I have heat' rather than 'I'm hot'. Here's a short list of similar expressions:

j'ai chaud – I'm hot   **j'ai faim** – I'm hungry
j'ai froid – I'm cold   **j'ai soif** – I'm thirsty
j'ai sommeil – I'm sleepy   **j'ai de la chance** – I'm lucky

110   cent dix

On appelle un taxi(?)	'Let's call a taxi/Shall we call a taxi?' It's sometimes reassuring to see that there's absolutely no spelling change involved in turning a statement into a question – just add a question mark and raise your voice at the end of the sentence!

Your turn 2

Here are some anagrams of several words and expressions used in the dialogue. Can you solve them?   ⊙ 78

1. diahujac ....
2. tasuhence ....
3. mamcerdon ....
4. nosibos ....
5. limomes ....

Can you say the following in French? Check your answers by listening to track 79.   ⊙ 79

1. I don't dance very well.
2. I'm going to the toilet.
3. I'm sleepy
4. Shall we call a taxi?

Make sure you've understood what is being said. Answer the following questions as you listen to the people talking: ⊙ 80

1. What is said about the group's singer? ....
2. What solution is suggested to relieve the heat? ....
3. How far away is the hotel? ....
4. When will they next see each other? ....

Look at the questions on the left and give the answers on the right.

This may seem a bit repetitive, but you're practising changing the endings of the verb forms. The first row has been completed to start you off.

1. **Tu veux** une pression?   Oui, **je veux** une pression.

2. **Tu danses** bien?   Oui, ... bien.

3. **Tu as** chaud?   Oui, ... chaud.

4. **Tu es** fatigué?   Oui, ... fatigué.

5. **Tu vas** au bar?   Oui, ... au bar.

 Let's recap

In this unit we've looked at various ways of making suggestions. Here are some model sentences to help you remember:

Allons au café.

On pourrait aller au café.

Tu veux aller au café?

We also learned some useful new expressions with *avoir*.

• •

Now see how good your memory is. Below are some English expressions – give the French for each, but in the negative form:

e.g. I'm sleepy   je **n'**ai **pas** sommeil

1. I'm from Lyon. ....

2. I want to have some champagne. ....

3. I'm thirty years old. ....

4. I'm going to the WC. ....

Choose the correct option to complete each sentence:

1. .... prendre un verre.

   a. Allons   **b.** Pourrait   **c.** Vous   **d.** C'est

2. On .... autre chose?

   a. boisson   **b.** prendre   **c.** commande   **d.** pression

3. Un groupe .... ce soir.

   a. jazz   **b.** est   **c.** jour   **d.** joue

4. .... appelle un taxi?

   a. Tu   **b.** Il y a   **c.** On   **d.** Voilà

Rester en contact

Keeping in touch

12

We'll consolidate what we've learned so far in the course, as well as looking ahead to meeting up with our new French friends in the future. To do this, we'll be having a look at the language of communication – phones, mobiles, texting and email.

Traveller's tip

It's great to make friends in France during your visit, and to keep in touch once you're back in your own country. It's an ideal way to practise the language, as well as giving you a social foundation for future visits.

These days, your mobile phone – **le mobile** or **le portable** – and email – **le courriel** or **l'e-mail** – are the two most common tools for keeping in touch. In fact, you may already have used email in France – in **un cybercafé** (internet café) – and may be used to phoning or texting home by mobile.

You'll see that French people are every bit as technologically savvy as foreign visitors, and that there are a range of telephony companies working in tandem with your mobile service provider back home. Don't be surprised if, when you switch on your cell phone on emerging from the airport in France, your screen lights up with the name of a local telephone network.

Roaming rates have dropped spectacularly over the last couple of years, but if you want to contact friends and family living in France while you're there on holiday, you also have the option of buying a French SIM card or even a cheap French mobile.

Cafés internet can be found in most French towns and cities, and rates tend to be very reasonable. You may even find your hotel has internet and Wifi facilities available to guests.

In this unit we'll be revising questions and answers in the context of making plans for the future, using the language of communication.

Tu m'enverras un e-mail? Will you send me an email?
Je t'enverrai un SMS. I'll send you a text.
Quel est ton numéro de téléphone? What's your phone number?

Listen up 1

Linda and Tom have reached the end of their holiday, and are swapping contact details with their new friend Michel. Listen out for two phone numbers and an email address. ◎ 81

The trio have a farewell drink together before Linda and Tom leave for the airport. You'll hear departure and arrival times for the flight, and a decision on how to get to the airport. ◎ 82

Transcripts for the audio tracks on the CD are available online at www.collinslanguage.com/click.

Words and phrases 1

Quel est ton numéro de téléphone?	What's your phone number?
Je vais te l'écrire	I'm going to jot it down for you.
mon numéro *m* de portable	my mobile number
je vais te donner	I'm going to give you (from **donner** – to give)
mon adresse *f* e-mail	my email address
dernier	last
ensemble	together
avion *m*	aeroplane
je vais vous accompagner	I'll come with you (lit. I'll accompany you).
prendre un taxi	to take a taxi

nous y allons	we're going there
c'est moins cher	it's cheaper (lit. it's less expensive)
quand même	anyway

 ## Unlocking the language 1

Quel est ton numéro de téléphone?

'What (lit. which) is your phone number?' Notice the word order – your number of telephone.

C'est le zéro quatre, soixante-quatorze, quarante-huit, **zéro six**, quatre-vingt-onze.

'It's 04-74-48-06-91.' The style of giving phone numbers in French takes a bit of getting used to. Firstly, 'it's' is **c'est le**.

Digits are stated in pairs – forty-eight, ninety-one, etc. A pair beginning with zero (e.g. 06) is pronounced **zéro six** *(zayro seess)*. These conventions take a bit of getting used to, so listen to the dialogue again and focus on how the numbers are given.

To call France from abroad you'll need the international code from your own country (00 from the UK), followed by 33 (**trente-trois**) for France. Then continue dialling the person's number, leaving out the first zero.

tom.simpson44@ myemail.co.uk

The convention for pronouncing an email address is: tom-**point**-simpson-quarante-quatre-**arobase**-myemail-**point**-co-**point**-u-k. The key words here are **point** for 'dot' and **arobase**, meaning 'at'. If there's no dot and you want to say 'all one word', use **en un mot**.

je vous accompagne

'I'll accompany you.' This structure is something we saw during Unit 11. 'French says' 'I you accompany'.

Je vais te l'écrire.

'I'm going to jot it down for you.'

Je vais te donner ...

'I'm going to give you ...'

Je vais vous accompagner.

'I'm going to accompany you.'

We saw this first in Unit 9 - in French, 'I'm going' is **je vais**. To say 'I'm going to do something', just add the basic form of a verb after **je vais**. 'I'm going eat' **je vais manger**, 'I'm going to order' **je vais commander**.

Find expressions in the dialogues to convey the following. The
answers to the activities in this booklet are available online at
www.collinslanguage.com/click

◉ 81–82

1. What's your phone number?

2. I'm going to jot it down for you.

3. Have you got a mobile?

4. I'm going to give you my email address.

5. I'm going to come with you to the airport.

6. Shall we take a taxi?

> ## Pronunciation Tip
>
> **Olivier, dernier, donner**
> We've seen a lot of words in this
> course with **-er** at the end. It is
> pronounced like **é**, and like *ay* in
> 'say'. **-ier** is then pronounced
> *yeah*, with a silent **-r**.

··

How would you say the following? Two answers are given to get
you started. Check your answers by listening to the audio track.

◉ 83

Mon numéro de téléphone est le ...

1. 03-36-45-67-02 – zéro trois, trente-six, quarante-cinq, soixante-sept, zéro deux

2. 01-19-84-56-02 – zéro un, dix-neuf, quatre-vingt-quatre, cinquante-six, zéro deux

3. 04-75-55-07-94 ....
   ....

4. 02-49-27-13-61 ....
   ....

5. 05-12-31-62-98 ....
   ....

Two French friends have given you their email addresses, but some 84 of the letters are missing. Try and write down the missing letters as you hear them.

Je vais te donner mon adresse e-mail:

1. gre_ _ry.ta_d_@y_h_ _.f_

2. ja_ _ues.d_m_s@ con _ _ c _ _ m_ i._ _ _

. . . .

Match the questions or suggestions on the left with the English translations on the right:

1. À quelle heure ...?   Have you got ...?

2. As-tu ...?   What's ...?

3. Quel est ...?   We could ...

4. Peux-tu m'écrire ...?   What time ...?

5. On pourrait ...   Can you jot ... down for me?

Listen up 2

Tom and Linda have reached the airport. Now it's time to say  85 goodbye to Michel. Listen out for more contact details, as well as various ways of saying goodbye.

Words and phrases 2

Tu m'enverras un SMS (un texto)?	Will you send me a text? there are three ways of saying 'text message' in French: **un texte, un texto** or **un SMS**.
de Londres	from London

Un quoi?	A what?
bien sûr	of course
ça y est	that's it
Je l'ai.	I've got it.
une photo *f*	photo
je t'enverrai ...	I'll send you ...
Je ne l'ai pas.	I don't have it.
Bon allez	Right then
Je t'embrasse	I'm giving you a kiss (on the cheeks). The number of kisses may be two, three, or even four – it depends on the region or city.
merci pour tout	thanks for everything
à une prochaine (fois)	'til next time
au plaisir de te revoir	bye-bye, see you (lit. to the pleasure to see you again)
À très bientôt.	See you very soon.
j'espère	I hope
à l'année prochaine	See you next year (lit. until the next year).
je vais vous rendre visite	I'm going to pay you a visit
bon voyage	safe journey/have a good trip
Au revoir	Bye (lit. until seeing again)

🔓 Unlocking the language 2

tu m'enverras
je t'enverrai
enverras is the **tu** form and **enverrai** is the **je** form of the future tense of **envoyer**, 'to send'. Notice that in French the future is a one-word tense, whereas in English it's a two-word tense: 'I will send'

à/à une/au/à l' ...
Literally meaning 'until', this is very useful when you want to say 'see you (at some point in the future)': **à demain** ('see you tomorrow'), **à bientôt** ('see you soon'), **à l'année prochaine** ('see you next year').

une année/un an
There are two words for 'year' in French: **année** is used to talk about calendar years – **l'année prochaine** ('next year'), whereas **an** is used for measuring time in years – **j'ai trente ans** ('I'm thirty').

Can you remember the expressions needed to construct this short ⊙ 85
dialogue in French? Refer to the dialogue if you need to.

1. Have you got my email address? ....

2. That's it, I've got it. ....

3. I'll send you the photos tomorrow. ....

4. Thanks for everything. ....

5. See you very soon. ....

6. Have a good trip. ....

Can you say the following in French? They're all fragments of ⊙ 86
language to do with communication. Check your answers by
listening to the audio track.

1. I haven't got a mobile.

2. It's ... (when introducing your phone number)

3. a mobile phone

4. dot (in an email address)

5. at (in an email address)

Listen to one person giving his email address, and another giving ⊙ 87
her phone number. Try and write them both down as you listen:

1. ....

2. ....

Write out these phone numbers in full. The first answer is given to get you started.

e.g. 01-47-82-31-69 zéro un, quarante-sept, quatre-vingt-deux, trente et un, soixante-neuf

1. 03-92-72-47-64 ....
....

2. 05-17-91-83-24 ....
....

3. 02-64-56-70-30 ....
....

4. 04-77-34-18-29 ....
....

⟳ Let's recap

In this unit we've looked at various structures to do with exchanging contact information. Here are some model sentences:

Mon numéro de téléphone est le zéro six, cinquante-quatre, quarante-deux, soixante-sept, zéro huit (06-54-42-67-08)

Mon adresse e-mail est julie-point-berthet-arobase-orange-point f-r (julie.berthet@orange.fr)

Now see how good your memory is. Can you remember how to say:

1. Have you got my email address?

2. I've got your mobile number.

3. Two ways of saying 'I'll send you a text'.

Put the words in the right order to make a sentence:

1. enverrai je un t' SMS ....

2. te l' vais je écrire ....

3. vais donner e-mail mon je adresse te ....

4. accompagner vous vais je ....

5. frites nous pouvez des donner vous? ....

6. en y bus allons nous ....

. . . .

Choose the correct option to complete each sentence:

1. Merci .... tout.

   a. de   b. pour   c. par   d. en

2. À l' .... prochaine.

   a. demain   b. visite   c. année   d. heure

3. Je vais vous .... visite.

   a. vouloir   b. préférer   c. avoir   d. rendre

4. .... voyage!

   a. Bon   b. Bonne   c. Bien   d. Bons

Révisions 2
Revision 2

Age

Remember that in French you 'have' an age, rather than 'being' it. Make sure you can say your age using *j'ai … ans*.

Listen to four people saying how old they are. Write down each person's age: ⦿ 88

1. Rachel: ....
2. Emmanuel: ....
3. Hélène: ....
4. Claude: ....

Tu and vous

Your use of the informal and polite versions of French verbs will depend very much on what sort of people you're mixing with and the formality of the situations you experience. It's a good idea to take some time out and listen again to all the dialogues we've covered, practising converting polite verbs to informal, and vice versa.

For a bit of practice, try changing the following polite forms into informal versions. The first one is done for you:

Polite	Informal
Voulez-vous une pression?	Veux-tu une pression?
Êtes-vous canadien?	....
Allez-vous à Marseille?	....
Avez-vous sommeil?	....
Parlez-vous français?	....

Shopping

You've seen that there are a lot of conventions in the language of shopping. Have a look back through the dialogues, and try substituting the items bought for items you'd be likely to buy in France. Make a vocabulary list to increase your confidence.

Speak out

⊙ 89

Can you remember how you'd say the following? Try saying the sentences out loud. Check your answers by listening to the audio track.

1. I'm looking for a white shirt.
2. How much is it?
3. It's a bit expensive.
4. I'll take it.

Likes and dislikes

Starting with the simple formula of **j'aime ...** or **je n'aime pas ...**, you can very easily cover your likes and dislikes. Remember that you don't have to limit this to items or concepts (**j'aime le café, j'aime l'art**); you can talk about activities too (**j'aime étudier**). Asking others about their preferences is easy, too: there's the informal **Aimes-tu ...?** or the polite **Aimez-vous ...?**

Listen to the people talking about their likes and dislikes, and answer the questions below:

⊙ 90

1. Charlotte likes white wine – true or false? ....
2. What does Xavier like doing? ....
3. Florence likes Paris very much – true or false? ....
4. Does Michel like working? ....

Communication

Write down all your contact details, then think about pronouncing everything in French. It's a good idea to write it all out 'longhand' – e.g. if your phone number begins 3348 then write down **trente-trois, quarante-huit**. This is especially important for your email address: remember the magic words **point** for 'dot' and **arobase** for '@'. Keep practising these until you find you can say them all fluently without referring to your paper.

Bonne chance!

Good luck!

HAVE YOU SEEN OUR FULL FRENCH RANGE? PICK A TITLE TO FIT YOUR LEARNING STYLE.

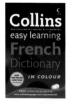

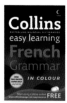

Collins Easy Learning Series

The bestselling language resources, perfect if you're learning French for the first time or brushing up on rusty language skills.

Dictionary
£8.99

Grammar
£6.99

Verbs
£6.99

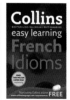

Words
£6.99

Complete 3-in-1 volume
£10.99

Conversation
£6.99

Idioms
£5.99

Collins Easy Learning Audio Courses

This exciting course allows learners to absorb the basics at home or on the move, without the need for thick textbooks or complex grammar.

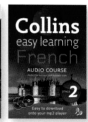

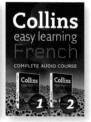

Audio Course stage 1
£9.99

Audio Course stage 2
£12.99

Complete Audio Course (1 and 2) £17.99